Moodle 2.5 Multimedia Cookbook

Second Edition

GW00597821

75 recipes to help you integrate different multimedia resources into your Moodle courses to make them more interactive

Silvina P. Hillar

[PACKT]
PUBLISHING

open source *
community experience distilled

BIRMINGHAM - MUMBAI

Moodle 2.5 Multimedia Cookbook
Second Edition

First published: May 2011

Second Edition: October 2013

Production Reference: 1181013

Published by Packt Publishing Ltd.
Livery Place
35 Livery Street
Birmingham B3 2PB, UK.

ISBN 978-1-78328-937-0

www.packtpub.com

Cover Image by Aleksandar Glisovic (gsorry@gmail.com)

Credits

Author

Silvina P. Hillar

Reviewers

Aparup Banerjee

Nicolas Dunand

Valery Guilhem Fremaux

Rajesh Taneja

Acquisition Editor

Joanne Fitzpatrick

Lead Technical Editor

Amey Varangaonkar

Technical Editors

Manan Badani

Pankaj Kadam

Pramod Kumavat

Krutika Parab

Hardik B. Soni

Project Coordinator

Angel Jathanna

Copy Editors

Tanvi Gaitonde

Gladson Monteiro

Sayanee Mukherjee

Adithi Shetty

Proofreader

Linda Morris

Indexer

Monica Ajmera Mehta

Production Coordinator

Aparna Bhagat

Cover Work

Aparna Bhagat

About the Author

Silvina P. Hillar is an Italian who has been teaching English since 1993. She has always had a great interest in teaching, writing, and composing techniques and has done a lot of research on this subject. She has been investigating and using mind mapping for more than ten years in order to embed it into teaching.

She is an English teacher, a Certified Legal Translator (English/Spanish), and has a Postgraduate degree in Education (graduated with Honors).

She has been working in several schools and institutes with native English speaking students, and as an independent consultant for many international companies working as an interpreter, translator, and VLE (Virtual Learning Environment) course designer.

She has always had a passion for technological devices concerning education. Former videos and cassettes were a must in her teaching lessons, and computer was, and still is, present. Her brother, Gastón C. Hillar, designed some programs and games for her teaching. Lately, she is teaching using Moodle and the Web 2.0. She believes that one of the most amazing challenges in education is bridging the gap between classic education and modern technologies.

She has been doing a lot of research on multimedia assets that enhance teaching and learning through VLE platforms. She tries to embed the learning of students through new resources which are appealing and innovative for them. Thus, multimedia stimulates different thinking skills, as well as multiple intelligences.

She has authored three books at Packt Publishing, which are Moodle 1.9: The English Teacher's Cookbook, Moodle 2 Multimedia Cookbook, and MindMapping with FreeMind.

Acknowledgments

I would like to thank all the team members at Packt Publishing Ltd. who worked with me as an incredibly helpful team, Joanne Fitzpatrick who trusted me to update this book—we worked together so that the idea came into this book—Angel Jathanna who was very patient and helpful with time management, and Amey Varangaonkar who also was an important part of this project.

I want to thank the reviewers of this book who helped with their comments: Aparup Banerjee, Nicolas Dunand, Valery Fremaux, and Rajesh Taneja, they were really helpful.

I also want to thank the technical editors who worked with me in the editing process of the book: Manan Badani, Pankaj Kadam, Pramod Kumavat, Krutika Parab, and Hardik B. Soni.

I owe tremendous thanks to my wonderful nine-year-old son, Nico, who despite his age was very patient and supportive in the writing process of the book. He was on some occasions forced to play and study alone while I concentrated on my writing.

My parents, Susana and Jose (who is also a writer), who always stand by me and support my decisions. My brother, Gastón C. Hillar, who helps me whenever I need him, as usual. My little four-year-old nephew Kevin, my newly born nephew Brandon, and my sister-in-law, Vanesa S. Olsen, with whom we spend time working and exploring Moodle, as well as many other resources.

I would also like to thank all my students, either real or virtual, who make it possible for me to be a teacher.

About the Reviewers

Aparup Banerjee holds a Bachelors in Applied Science in Computer Engineering from NTU, Singapore. He has been in the IT industry for over 15 years. He is happily married in Australia with two inquisitive bright young children and shares the passions of the education industry and social constructivism with his lovely wife Indu.

He has spent the past several years in Moodle "HQ" wearing the hat of a developer, as well as in qualitative roles, carefully reviewing, testing, and integrating changes to the final Moodle software product. He currently helps facilitate and maintain the Moodle Plugins Directory, as well as developing and maintaining other Moodle.org sites. This has brought about a specialization in the education industry, particularly with online delivery and Moodle.

Nicolas Dunand is a systems administrator and Moodle specialist for a higher educational institution, where he is responsible for the administration and custom development of Moodle. He is the maintainer and a contributor of various Moodle plugins. He is also a self-employed web developer and works on private projects ranging from websites to online databases, including secure delivery of confidential documents.

Valery Guilhem Fremaux is one of the leading French Moodle technical experts and a noticeable Moodle contributor for about 10 years. He worked on public statewide programs using Moodle as the core LCMS environment in big size deployment projects (> 800,000 users), and he administrates about 100 Moodle applications for many public and private schools and professional development institutions. Nowadays, he works as an independent consultant dealing with digital learning and Moodle integration,

He has taught at EISTI (Graduate Engineer Degree in IT and Data Technologies) for 13 years and managed the Applied Studies Laboratories in the IT department of the school.

Valery Fremaux has authored and contributed to many IT-related books in France, such as Java basics (Ellipses), Java advanced (Ellipses), a Roger Pressman 5th Edition free adaptation in French (Ellipses), and the WAP forum translation (Eyrolles).

Rajesh Taneja is an experienced software developer with over 10 years of hands-on experience in various IT technologies and languages. He has worked across the world for renowned companies such as Mentor Graphics, Samsung, Calorie King, and Moodle to name a few. He has a passion and a knack to learn and hone technologies. Currently, he is an Analyst Developer at Moodle Headquarters in Perth, Australia and also provides consultancy to various learning organizations. Rajesh loves gardening and working on DIY projects in his spare time only when his toddler son Ansh permits him to do so. You can contact Rajesh through his LinkedIn profile `http://www.linkedin.com/in/rajeshtaneja` or e-mail him on `rajesh.taneja@gmail.com`.

First and foremost, I want to thank my wife, Deepti, for all of the support and encouragement she has given. My son Ansh, who will be turning five soon, has also shown patience when his dad was reviewing the book.

www.PacktPub.com

Support files, eBooks, discount offers and more

You might want to visit `www.PacktPub.com` for support files and downloads related to your book.

Did you know that Packt offers eBook versions of every book published, with PDF and ePub files available? You can upgrade to the eBook version at `www.PacktPub.com` and as a print book customer, you are entitled to a discount on the eBook copy. Get in touch with us at `service@packtpub.com` for more details.

At `www.PacktPub.com`, you can also read a collection of free technical articles, sign up for a range of free newsletters and receive exclusive discounts and offers on Packt books and eBooks.

`http://PacktLib.PacktPub.com`

Do you need instant solutions to your IT questions? PacktLib is Packt's online digital book library. Here, you can access, read and search across Packt's entire library of books.

Why Subscribe?

- ► Fully searchable across every book published by Packt
- ► Copy and paste, print and bookmark content
- ► On demand and accessible via web browser

Free Access for Packt account holders

If you have an account with Packt at `www.PacktPub.com`, you can use this to access PacktLib today and view nine entirely free books. Simply use your login credentials for immediate access.

Dedicated to my beloved son, Nico

Table of Contents

Preface   **1**

Chapter 1: Creating Interactive User eXperiences   **7**

Introduction   7

Creating a cloze with pictures   8

Designing a True/False quiz   13

Developing a quandary maze activity with images   21

Designing matching activities with pictures   24

Ordering paragraphs with related scenes   29

Creating storyboards   31

Embedding the story in Moodle   35

Embedding the Fakebook of William Shakespeare   37

Chapter 2: Working with 2D and 3D Maps   **43**

Introduction   43

Using maps with sceneries   45

Drawing regions within a map   47

Using weather maps   50

Using Google Maps to locate European bridges   53

Working with Yahoo! Maps   55

Watching stars through Bing Maps 3D   57

Drawing 3D maps using 3DVIA Shape for Maps   61

Working with constellation maps   66

Embedding a map of Mars   68

Labeling the moon   71

Watching the universe   73

Chapter 3: Working with Different Types of Interactive Charts — 77

Introduction — 77
Inserting column charts — 78
Embedding a line chart — 81
Designing a graph out of a choice activity — 85
Creating bar charts with hyperlinks — 86
Working with area charts — 92
Creating a poll and designing a surface chart — 96
Drawing a donut interactive chart — 99
Designing a map chart — 102
Creating a gauge chart — 104

Chapter 4: Integrating Interactive Documents — 109

Introduction — 109
Developing collaborative writing exercises with Google Docs — 110
Using Flickr images in OpenOffice documents — 113
Including live PDF documents in Moodle — 117
Using Google Drive Voice Comments for online assignments — 121
Designing a collaborative wiki — 125
Sharing files with Office 365 Education — 130
Sharing a folder from Dropbox — 134
Working with files and folders within Moodle — 136

Chapter 5: Working with Audio, Sound, Music, and Podcasts — 139

Introduction — 139
Recording audio from a microphone — 141
Creating and embedding a podcast using SoundCloud — 145
Using VoiceThread to record presentations — 149
Embedding a presentation in VoiceThread using Moodle — 152
Using LibriVox to embed an audiobook — 154
Allowing students to record audio — 158

Chapter 6: Creating and Integrating Videos — 161

Introduction — 161
Recording a video — 162
Uploading a video on YouTube — 165
Editing a video using a YouTube editor — 167
Embedding a Vimeo video — 173
Enhancing a video with comments — 179
Creating and embedding a Prezi presentation — 183
Creating a playlist — 186
Creating an animated video using Wideo — 189

Chapter 7: Working with Bitmaps and Photographs   193

Introduction   193
Selecting between lossy and lossless compression schemes   194
Resizing photos to their appropriate size   197
Adding hotspots to photos   200
Editing color curves   204
Adding effects and applying filters   206
Uploading images to Moodle   211
Creating animated 3D graphics   213
Linking external image files from thinglink.com   216
Embedding images from thinglink.com   220

Chapter 8: Working with Vector Graphics   223

Introduction   223
Converting vector graphics to bitmap images   224
Converting bitmaps to vector graphics   227
Rendering parts of a converted vector drawing   230
Embedding scalable vector graphics   235
Improving vector graphics rendering with anti-aliasing   237
Including vector graphics in OpenOffice documents   239
Including vector graphics in PDF files   244
Enhancing scalable vector graphics with hyperlinks   245

Chapter 9: Designing and Integrating Repositories and E-portfolios   249

Introduction   249
Enabling the Box.net repository   250
Working with Box.net   254
Enabling the Flickr repository   256
Working with Flickr   260
Enabling portfolios   263
Enabling the File Download portfolio   265
Working with the Alfresco repository   268
Enabling the Alfresco repository   271

Index   275

Preface

Moodle is an open source, cross-platform virtual learning environment that is widely used in schools and businesses, specifically multimedia elements to enhance the user experience. Moodle as a Course Management System helps to create online courses with the major focus being on interaction.

Moodle 2.5 Multimedia Cookbook consists of recipes, which give information on how to design activities using multimedia resources. Besides, using special hardware devices to execute activities is also covered in this book. Learn how to use the most modern hardware devices with Moodle. Take advantage of these hardware devices to access your courses with multimedia content and rich activities.

It also provides a practical step-by-step guide to build and complete a multimedia course in Moodle 2.5, starting with creating interactive User eXperiences and ending with enabling and organizing work in e-portfolios.

It will help you to link, edit, and embed bitmaps and photographs; learn to resize and convert them to the most appropriate formats for Moodle courses, interactive documents, and e-portfolios. Work with animated graphics to create engaging activities and learn the most complex topics related to formats, compression, bitmaps, and vector graphics while following steps in simple recipes.

Moodle 2.5 Multimedia Cookbook teaches you how to work with free and open source software and services to perform most of the activities explained in the recipes.

What this book covers

We will cover the following chapters in this book:

Chapter 1, Creating Interactive User eXperiences, explains how to create rich activities for our Moodle courses. It will also cover working with graphics to create engaging activities for students, as graphics tend to be an important asset to bear in mind when designing an activity.

Chapter 2, Working with 2D and 3D Maps, explains how to create and embed different types of 2D and 3D interactive maps in Moodle courses. The recipes use web resources, as well as free and open source software to build and display interactive maps. Working with weather maps available on the Web is a new feature of the update.

Chapter 3, Working with Different Types of Interactive Charts, explains how to create and embed different types of 2D and 3D interactive and static charts in Moodle courses. The recipes use diverse tools and techniques to display data in charts and to provide students with the necessary information for their activities.

Chapter 4, Integrating Interactive Documents, explains how to use diverse types of interactive documents in Moodle courses. The recipes use the most popular free, commercial, web-based, and desktop-based software to create interactive documents for Moodle courses and provide students with the necessary information for their research activities.

Chapter 5, Working with Audio, Sound, Music, and Podcasts, explains how to work with different types of audio files to offer sounds, music, and podcasts in our Moodle courses. The recipes use diverse tools to record, edit, and convert the different audio files, covering the most common scenarios for multimedia Moodle activities.

Chapter 6, Creating and Integrating Videos, explains how to create screencasts and to edit, link, and embed videos for our Moodle courses. The recipes use diverse free and open source multiplatform tools to record, edit, and convert the different video files, covering the most common scenarios for multimedia Moodle activities.

Chapter 7, Working with Bitmaps and Photographs, explains how to work with different types of image file formats that use lossless and lossy compression schemes. The recipes use diverse tools to edit, enhance, and convert the different image files, covering the most common scenarios for multimedia Moodle activities.

Chapter 8, Working with Vector Graphics, explains how to work with different types of vector graphics formats. The recipes use diverse free and open source tools to edit, enhance, and convert the different vector graphics files, covering the most common scenarios for multimedia Moodle activities. Vector graphics are one of the most difficult formats to handle in Moodle courses.

Chapter 9, Designing and Integrating Repositories and E-portfolios, explains how to design and integrate e-portfolios in Moodle courses. We are also going to learn exciting techniques to organize information for students, as well as combine everything learned so far in interactive e-portfolios.

What you need for this book

As requirements or prerequisites, readers need previous basic experience with Moodle 1.9 and 2.x, as well as the installation and configuration procedures.

Who this book is for

Moodle 2.5 Multimedia Cookbook is designed for teachers who want to learn to insert different multimedia assets in their Moodle courses to make them more interactive. Teachers of different subjects can use the recipes to create the activities to cover a specific subject or topic. This book is also meant for the Moodlers who would like to enhance their Moodle courses through the use of new multimedia resources. As a prerequisite, basic knowledge of Moodle 1.9 and 2.x, as well as the installation and configuration procedures, is expected.

Conventions

In this book, you will find a number of styles of text that distinguish between different kinds of information. Here are some examples of these styles, and an explanation of their meaning.

Code words in text, database table names, folder names, filenames, file extensions, pathnames, dummy URLs, user input, and Twitter handles are shown as follows: "Create a new folder on your computer, for example, `C:\Images_Nobelprize`."

A block of code is set as follows:

```
<p><img src=
"http://localhost/draftfile.php/5/user/draft/317291260/Garfield_iPads.
JPG" alt="iPad_Garfield_app" height="750" width="1000" />
</p>
```

When we wish to draw your attention to a particular part of a code block, the relevant lines or items are set in bold:

```
<p>
<img src=
"http://localhost/draftfile.php/5/user/draft/317291260/Garfield_iPads.
JPG" alt="iPad_Garfield_app" height="750" width="1000" usemap="#map"
border="0"/>
</p>
```

New terms and **important words** are shown in bold. Words that you see on the screen, in menus or dialog boxes for example, appear in the text like this: "Right-click on the image and click on **Save picture as...**, as shown in the following screenshot."

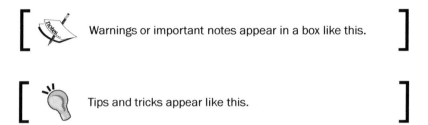

Reader feedback

Feedback from our readers is always welcome. Let us know what you think about this book—what you liked or may have disliked. Reader feedback is important for us to develop titles that you really get the most out of.

To send us general feedback, simply send an e-mail to feedback@packtpub.com, and mention the book title via the subject of your message.

If there is a topic that you have expertise in and you are interested in either writing or contributing to a book, see our author guide on www.packtpub.com/authors.

Customer support

Now that you are the proud owner of a Packt book, we have a number of things to help you to get the most from your purchase.

Downloading the example code

You can download the example code files for all Packt books you have purchased from your account at http://www.packtpub.com. If you purchased this book elsewhere, you can visit http://www.packtpub.com/support and register to have the files e-mailed directly to you.

Errata

Although we have taken every care to ensure the accuracy of our content, mistakes do happen. If you find a mistake in one of our books—maybe a mistake in the text or the code—we would be grateful if you would report this to us. By doing so, you can save other readers from frustration and help us improve subsequent versions of this book. If you find any errata, please report them by visiting http://www.packtpub.com/submit-errata, selecting your book, clicking on the **errata submission form** link, and entering the details of your errata. Once your errata are verified, your submission will be accepted and the errata will be uploaded on our website, or added to any list of existing errata, under the Errata section of that title. Any existing errata can be viewed by selecting your title from http://www.packtpub.com/support.

Piracy

Piracy of copyright material on the Internet is an ongoing problem across all media. At Packt, we take the protection of our copyright and licenses very seriously. If you come across any illegal copies of our works, in any form, on the Internet, please provide us with the location address or website name immediately so that we can pursue a remedy.

Please contact us at copyright@packtpub.com with a link to the suspected pirated material.

We appreciate your help in protecting our authors, and our ability to bring you valuable content.

Questions

You can contact us at questions@packtpub.com if you are having a problem with any aspect of the book, and we will do our best to address it.

1
Creating Interactive User eXperiences

In this chapter, we will cover the following recipes:

- ▶ Creating a cloze with pictures
- ▶ Designing a True/False quiz
- ▶ Developing a quandary maze activity with images
- ▶ Designing matching activities with pictures
- ▶ Ordering paragraphs with related scenes
- ▶ Creating storyboards
- ▶ Embedding the story in Moodle
- ▶ Embedding the Fakebook of William Shakespeare

Introduction

There are many ways to build or create rich interactive user experiences to enhance our Moodle course. Therefore, we will learn how to design them using a combination of technologies, free and open source software, and services available on the Web.

The chapter explains how to create rich activities for Moodle courses. We are also going to work with graphics to create engaging activities for our students. Also, note that images tend to be an important asset to bear in mind when designing an activity.

The aim of this chapter is to insert in our Moodle course the available applications in Web 2.0 in order to enrich our activities. Some of the software that we will use are Hot Potatoes, JClic, and Quandary 2; these are visually rich free software available on the Web. We can design activities using interactive websites as well.

There are also websites where we can design resources in order to embed them in our Moodle courses. Therefore, when we add them into the Moodle course we add a great ingredient to our activities. We have to take advantage of it in order to facilitate our work.

In this book we will create course materials, which deal with the subject of general knowledge. The topics will be different for each chapter. This chapter deals with Nobel Prize winners and people of achievement. We can find Nobel Prize winners on the website `http://nobelprize.org/`.

Creating a cloze with pictures

In this recipe, we create a cloze (Hot Potatoes activity) with images. We will deal with a Nobel Prize winner and write his biography using images. Students write the correct name for those images and they name the person afterwards. The idea is that the images are to be relevant to both the biography and the work carried out by the Nobel Prize winner. By the way, you are not going to be given the name of the person until the end of this activity!

Getting ready

In this activity, we use Hot Potatoes and create an activity using **JCloze**. You can download Hot Potatoes software from its website `http://hotpot.uvic.ca/#downloads`. In order to enable Hot Potatoes in our Moodle course, our Moodle administrator needs to install a plugin.

 Hot Potatoes is freeware, whose suite includes six applications, enabling you to create interactive multiple-choice, short-answer, jumbled-sentence, crossword, matching/ordering, and gap-fill exercises for the World Wide Web.

How to do it...

First of all, we have to choose the person to write about. You can choose a Nobel Prize winner from the website `http://nobelprize.org/`. Then, we read the biography (you can find a more detailed biography from the website `http://www.famouspeoplebiographyguide.com`) and design the gap-filling exercise.

We design the activity in such a way that students are given a clue with a picture in the gap, where they have to write the word. We have to find pictures in order to be able to design the activity. We look for the free clipart in Office Online Clip Art & Media at `http://office.microsoft.com/en-us/images/`; another interesting and suitable website is `http://www.openclipart.org/`.

Follow these steps to create a folder and find images for the activity:

1. Create a new folder on your computer, for example, `C:\Images_Nobelprize`.

2. Open your web browser and go to the aforementioned website.

3. Write the word `Baby` in the textbox and click on the search button, as shown in the following screenshot:

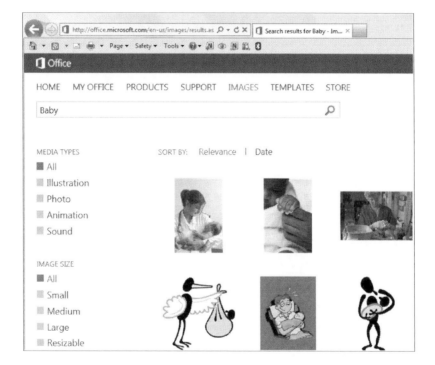

4. Double-click on the desired clipart or picture. The picture will appear in another bigger window.

5. Right-click on the image and click on **Save picture as...**, as shown in the following screenshot:

6. Save the picture in the folder that we created in step 1.

7. Repeat steps 2 to 6 in order to look for more images relevant to the biography of the person chosen.

How it works...

We have looked for images to insert in our activity. Therefore, let's use them! It is time to create the cloze using our images, so we have to run the Hot Potatoes software and click on **JCloze** (the blue potato). Then, follow these steps to design the activity:

1. Complete the **Title** block.

2. Write the biography of the person. Highlight the word where you want to create a gap.

3. Click on **Gap** when you want to add one, as shown in the following screenshot:

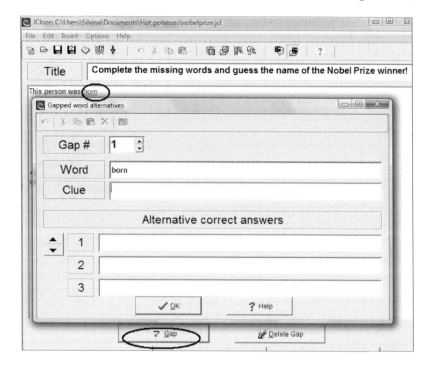

4. The circled underlined word is the one that is to be missing in the activity.

5. You can add clues if you want or any alternative words. Then, click on **OK**.

6. Click on **File | Save**, and save the file in the folder that we created to save the images.

7. Insert the image to give a visual clue to the gap. Position the cursor where you want to insert the image. Click on **Insert | Picture | Picture from Local File**, as shown in the following screenshot:

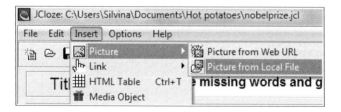

8. Choose the picture that you want to insert, click on **Open** (you can modify the width, height, and its adjustment), and then click on **OK**. You will not see the image, you will see an HTML code in the textbox.

9. Click on **File | Create Web Page | Standard Format**, and click on **Save**. Then, click on **View the exercise in my browser**. You will see the activity, as shown in the following screenshot:

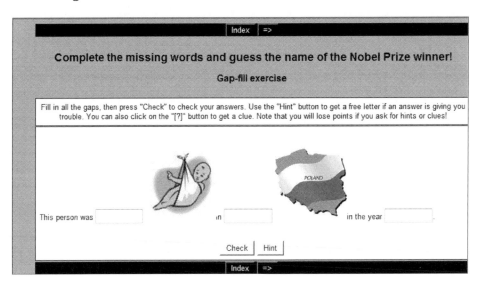

This is just a part of the cloze. We need to add more images to give more clues to the students, so that they can guess the name of this Nobel Prize winner.

There's more...

Now, we can upload the activity that we have just created in our Moodle course, but before doing it, our Moodle administrator has to install in the HotPot plugin following the instructions from the Moodle.org website. After installing and enabling the plugin, we can upload the activity in our Moodle course.

Uploading the activity in Moodle

We enter our Moodle course and choose the weekly outline section or the topic where we want to upload the activity. There are some steps that we have to follow:

1. Click on **Add an activity or resource**.

2. Click on **HotPot | Add**, as shown in the following screenshot:

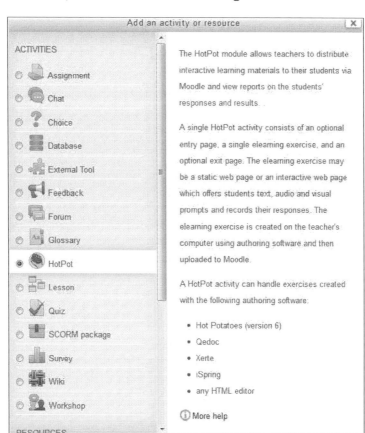

3. Click on **Add** to look for the file to upload.

4. Click on **Upload a file | Browse | Look for the file to upload (HTML) | Open | Upload this file**.

5. Repeat step 4 to upload the images inserted in the HotPot activity.

6. Click on **Save** and return to the course, the HotPot activity is ready.

Designing a True/False quiz

In this activity, we will design a True/False quiz. It is not an ordinary one though. We will create a guessing activity in which students decide whether the answers are either positive or negative and in that way they try to guess the name of another Nobel Prize winner. So, let's get ready.

Getting ready

First of all, we have to choose the Nobel Prize winner that we want our students to guess. Then, we design an activity using Moodle and insert images into our course, which is the multimedia asset in this recipe. Another possibility is to design the same activity using Hot Potatoes **JQuiz** (the yellow potato).

How to do it...

We design a guessing activity, but first we have to choose the Nobel Prize winner to work with; we have to bear in mind what type of information we want our students to guess. Therefore, we can insert images in the questions. So, in this case, we use free clipart from the website http://www.free-clipart-pictures.net.

In this recipe, we will design a True/False activity in our Moodle course. Choose the weekly outline section where we want to insert our activity and follow these steps:

1. Click on **Add an activity or resource | Quiz | Add**.
2. Complete the **Name** and **Description** blocks.
3. Click on **Save and display**.
4. Click on **Edit quiz**, as shown in the following screenshot:

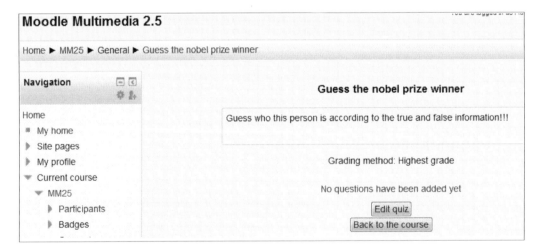

5. Click on **Add a question...**.
6. A pop-up window displaying different types of questions will appear, choose **True/False** and click on **Next**, as shown in the following screenshot:

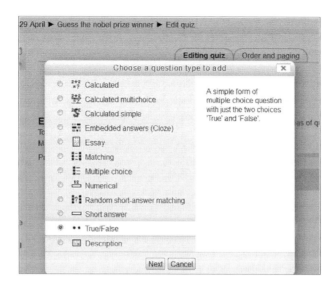

7. Complete the **Question text** block.

8. Open your web browser and enter the website `http://www.free-clipart-pictures.net`.

9. Click on **Child Clipart**. You have to look for the URL of the clipart to save it.

10. Right-click on the chosen clipart and click on **Properties**, as shown in the following screenshot:

11. If you are a Windows user, a pop-up window appears with the URL address of the image. We are going to highlight it, then right-click and copy it, as shown in the following screenshot:

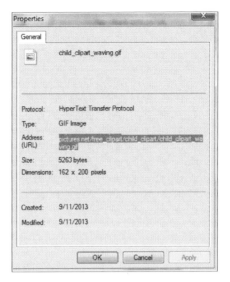

12. Click on **OK**.

13. Go back to your Moodle course. Click on the **Insert/edit image** icon to link to the existing image.

14. Complete the pop-up window, as shown in the following screenshot:

15. Click on **Insert**.

16. We can add information in the **Question text** block.

17. Complete the **Feedback for the response 'True'** and **Feedback for the response 'False'** blocks. You can add the correct images instead of writing. For example, if the person is not a woman, you can insert the image of a girl and a cross; if the person is a man, you can insert the image of the boy with a tick. It will give additional data.

18. Click on **Save changes**.

19. Click on **Add a question... | True/False | Next**.

20. Repeat steps 5 to 19 in order to add more questions to your quiz activity. Add as many questions as necessary. When there is no need to add more questions, go back to the course.

How it works...

Students are going to attempt the True/False quiz; after the results of the clues, they have to guess the name of the Nobel Prize winner. You may supply the name of the person in the last question of the activity. By the way, in this case, the Nobel Prize winner is John F. Nash Jr. The activity looks as is shown in the following screenshot:

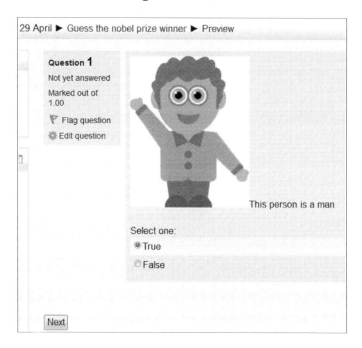

There's more...

We can also design the same activity using Hot Potatoes. This software also allows us to design True/False quizzes. Therefore, we open Hot Potatoes and click on **JQuiz**. Follow these steps and start designing the guessing activity:

1. Complete the **Title** block.

2. Choose **Multiple-choice** in the drop-down menu that appears on the top of the right hand margin.

3. Write the statement in the **Q1** block.

4. Write **True** and click on **Accept as correct** within **Settings**.

5. Write **False** on the next one, as shown in the following screenshot:

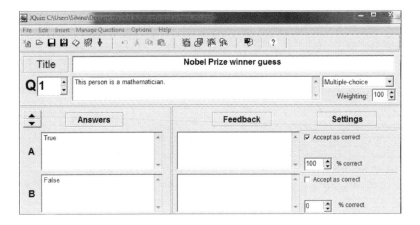

6. Click on the downward arrow next to **Q1**, and **Q2** will appear. Go on adding sentences to give tips to your students.

7. Save the file.

8. Click on **File | Create a web page | Standard Format | Save | View the exercise in my browser**.

9. You can also add any images to the activity by following the steps in the previous recipe.

10. Upload the activity in the Moodle course, as explained in the previous recipe. (Bear in mind that the HotPot module has to be installed by the Moodle administrator.)

More Info

We can also design a True/False activity using `http://testmoz.com/`. It is an interactive web page where you can easily design this quiz. We can upload this activity in our Moodle course under **Add an activity or resource** selecting **URL**. The website corrects the quiz by itself.

To create an interactive activity using Testmoz, navigate to `http://testmoz.com/`. Follow these steps to create an interactive True/False quiz:

1. Click on **Make a Test**.

2. Complete the **Test name** block.

3. Write a password, and then click on **Continue**.

4. Click on **Settings** and complete the settings blocks. Then click on **Save**.

5. Click on **Add New Question**.

6. Click on the drop-down menu in **Type** and choose **True/false**. Write the question in the **Question** block.

7. Click on **Save and Add New Question**, as shown in the following screenshot:

8. When you finish adding questions, click on **Save | Publish | Publish**.

9. Go back to the Moodle course to link the quiz and choose the weekly outline section to add the resource. Click on **Add an activity or resource | URL | Add**.

10. Complete the **Name** and **Description** blocks. Remember to write the passcode, otherwise students won't be able to work on the quiz.

11. Copy and paste the URL of the quiz in the **External URL** block.

12. Click on **Save and return to course**.

13. When students click on the activity they will have to provide their name and the passcode, as shown in the following screenshot:

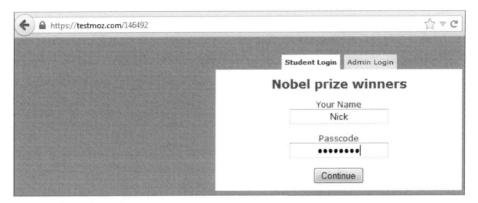

14. When they click on **Continue**, they can take the quiz, as shown in the following screenshot:

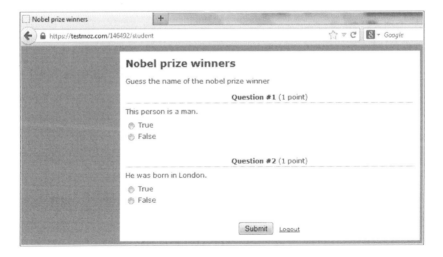

 We should bear in mind that the quiz results from Testmoz won't get passed back to Moodle, therefore they won't be included in the students' gradebook. However, it is an alternative to use in our Moodle courses in order to change the type of designing a True/False activity.

Developing a quandary maze activity with images

In this activity, we create a quandary maze using Quandary 2, which is a free and open source software. The only disadvantage is that it is only available for Windows. You can download it from `http://www.halfbakedsoftware.com/quandary.php`.

The quandary maze is about two people of achievement and a special animal. The three of them share a common characteristic. Students should guess their names by the clues given, and at the end of the maze they are going to figure out who they are. The idea is that they do not know who they are until the end of the maze in order to keep the mystery.

Getting ready

First of all, we have to download and install Quandary 2. Then, we have to think of two people of achievement and an animal who share a common characteristic. We need to deal with shared data so as to mislead students through our quandary activity. Thus, in some instances share the decision points or go back to another item.

We are going to upload images in this activity, so we create a new folder, for example, `C:\Images_PeopleofAchievement`. We will save all the images in this folder that we choose to design in our activity.

How to do it...

Open Quandary 2. The title of the activity is: People of Achievement and a Special Animal. Students choose different decision points, and they will have to guess whose biography they are reading. They are provided with different clues, both by text or images.

We will design this activity with images, and therefore navigate to `http://commons.wikimedia.org`, wherein there are many clipart pictures to work with. We search for images that we want to insert in the activity and save them in the folder that we have already created.

Open Quandary 2 and follow these steps in order to develop this activity:

1. Create a folder in which we are going to save both the file and the images that we are going to work with.
2. Click on **File** and select **New file**.
3. Click on **File | Save As**. Save the file in the folder that we have just created.
4. Complete the **Exercise Title**, **Decision Point title**, and **Decision Point contents** blocks.

5. Click on **New Link**; click on the drop-down box in the pop-up window and select **Create a new decision point**.

6. Complete the new block, and on **OK**.

7. Place the cursor in the **Link text** block and click on the **Insert a picture as the link, or part of the link** icon. Click on **Picture from local file**, as shown in the following screenshot:

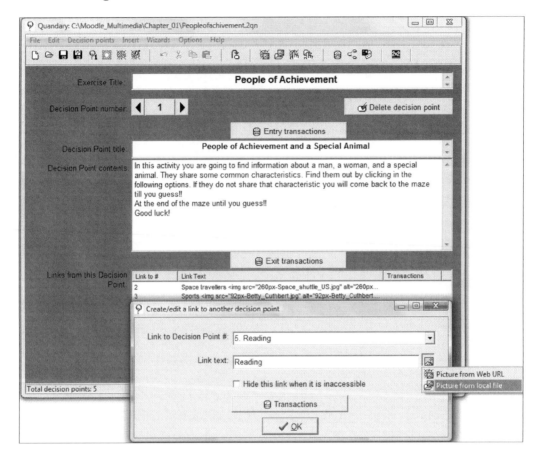

8. Browse for the picture within the folder that you have created. Click on **Open | OK | OK**.

9. Insert two or more new links in the same way. Therefore, repeat steps 5 to 8 in order to create more decision points.

10. Click on the right arrow on the left-hand side of the margin **Decision Point number** and the number changes to **2**. Go over the same process making the maze, guiding the students to know who they are.

11. When you finish, click on **File | Save file**.

12. Click on **File** and select **Export to XHTML**, as shown in the following screenshot:

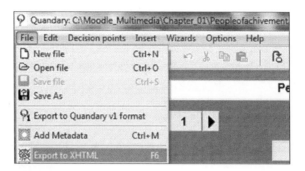

How it works...

We have finished designing our quandary activity, so it is time for our students to enjoy it. We need to upload the activity in our Moodle course. We upload the quandary activity through the HotPot module, so we choose the weekly outline section where we want to upload the activity and follow these steps:

1. Click on **Add an activity or resource**.

2. Click on **HotPot | Add**.

3. Click on **Add**.

4. Click on **Upload a file | Browse | Click on the file to upload (choose the .htm extension) | Open | Upload this file**.

5. Repeat step 4 to upload the images in the file.

6. Click on **Save and display**, the activity looks as shown in the following screenshot:

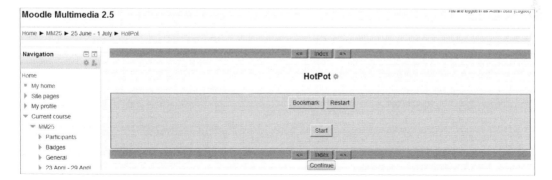

By the way, their names are Valentina Vladimirovna Tereshkova, Yuri Alekseyevich Gagarin, and Laika, the first dog in space.

Designing matching activities with pictures

In this activity, we will be working with another application available on the Web. It is a free and open source software called **JClic author 0.2.0.5**. So, the first thing that we have to do is to install it.

We will create a matching activity with images. You can also carry out this activity using either Moodle or JMatch within Hot Potatoes, which was already used in previous recipes.

We are going to design a matching activity with pictures. We choose 16 people of achievement and their main characteristic will be labeled by an icon image. So, the students have to match each person with the achievement that they are famous for. Can you think of so many talented people? Let's get ready!

Getting ready

We are going to work with JClic author, but if you don't have it installed you can download it from `http://clic.xtec.cat/en/jclic/download.htm`. You have to click on the **JClic author** icon and download the software following the steps mentioned.

After the installation, we work with images from `http://commons.wikimedia.org`. We create a folder (as we have already done in the previous activities), in which we save all the icon images that we have chosen, which represent these special people.

How to do it...

After thinking of 16 people of achievement and finding their icon images that you have saved in the folder (created for this activity), we have to design the activity in JClic author. Therefore, these are the steps that you have to follow:

1. Open JClic author. Select **File | New project...** and complete the pop-up window, as shown in the following screenshot:

2. Save the activity in the folder that you have created and saved the images in. Then, click on **OK**.

3. Click on **Project** and complete the **Title** and **Description** blocks, writing what students have to do in this activity.

4. Click on **Activities** and select **Insert | New activity...**. Select **Complex association**, as shown in the following screenshot:

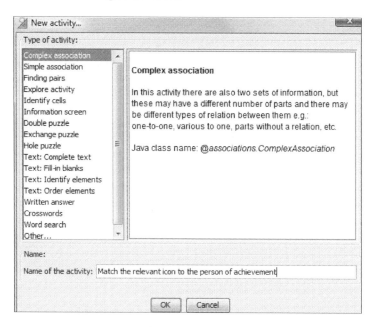

5. Write the name of the activity, as shown in the previous screenshot. Then, click on **OK**.

6. Complete the blocks related to **Options**, as you want the activity to be displayed.

7. Then, click on **Window** to customize it yourself or keep it as it is. There are many options for you to work with.

8. You can also choose to design the messages by clicking on **Messages**.

9. Click on **Panel** to design the activity. **Grid A** is the grid on the left, in which you write the names of the people of achievement. **Grid B** is the grid on the right, used to insert the icon images.

10. Click on **Grid A** and complete the options, as shown in the following screenshot. Therefore, you can insert 16 names by clicking in each cell and completing the pop-up window that appears for each of them. You only need to enter text on this grid:

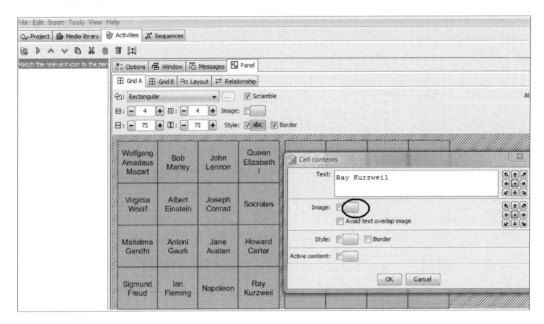

11. Click on **Grid B** to insert the icon images. Click on a cell, and then click on the big rectangle next to **Image**, as shown circled in the previous screenshot.

12. A new pop-up window will appear. Click on **New media object...** and choose the image that you want to use. Click on **Open | OK | OK**. The image will appear inside the cell.

13. Repeat the same process 15 times more, because we have inserted 16 people of achievement! Another option is to choose fewer items to connect.

14. Select **File | Save** to save the changes made.

15. Choose **View | Preview activity**. We can work out the activity, can't we?

How it works...

Now that we have designed the activity in JClic author, insert the previously created activity in our Moodle course. There is no module or block available in Moodle 2.5 to insert JClic activities, this is the reason why we have to make a link to the said file.

Follow these steps to prepare the activity in order to upload it to Moodle afterwards:

1. Click on **Tools | Create web page...**, as shown in the following screenshot:

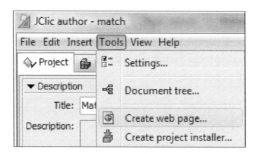

2. A pop-up window appears. Click on **OK | Save | Yes**.

3. The activity is ready to work with. It's time to upload it to our Moodle course.

Add this matching activity as a resource in the course. It can be the warm up activity to the introduction of any topic to deal with. Therefore, choose the weekly outline section where you want to place the activity and follow these steps:

1. Click on **Add an activity or resource | File | Add**.

2. Complete the **Name** and **Description** blocks.

3. In the **Content** section, click on **Add | Upload a file | Browse** and look for the file to upload in Moodle. Look for the `.htm` file that was previously created.

4. Click on **Open | Upload this file**.

5. Repeat steps 3 and 4 to upload the `.jclic.zip` file, as shown in the following screenshot:

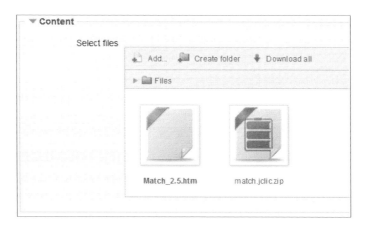

6. Click on **Save and display**. The JClic activity is ready to work with within Moodle!

There's more...

We can add another activity after this one. Use this matching activity as a lead to a writing one, for example, or as a warm up for a special assignment. We can add an online text activity so that, for instance, students give their reasons on who the most amazing person is and why.

Creating a writing activity

We can create a writing activity using the previous one designed in JClic author as a prewriting one. Thus, follow these steps to insert this new one in our Moodle course:

1. Click on **Add an activity or resource | Assignment | Add**.

2. Complete the **Assignment name** and **Description** blocks.

3. Within **Submission types**, select **File submissions**, as shown in the following screenshot:

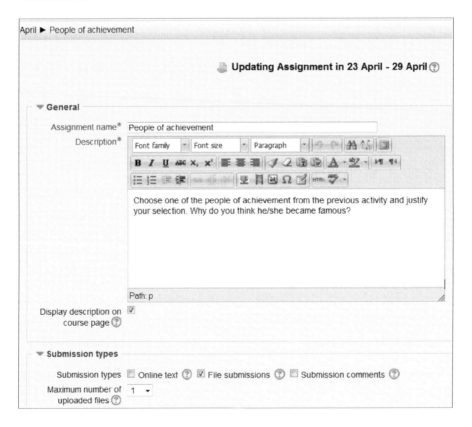

4. Click on **Save and return to course**.

Ordering paragraphs with related scenes

We can design this type of activity using several external software or tools available in Web 2.0. You can use JMatch within Hot Potatoes or a matching activity within JClic author. But we are not going to use those because we have already used them in earlier recipes. However, we can design an interactive timeline using `http://www.readwritethink.org/search/?sort_order=relevance&q=timeline&old_q=` or we can also design it using Microsoft Word or OpenOffice with images in it.

Getting ready

Enter the aforementioned website and click on **Timeline** so that we can design the timeline of a Nobel Prize winner. By the way, can you guess who we are going to work with?

How to do it...

Another screen will appear displaying the type of timeline that we are going to develop. So, these are the steps to follow:

1. Click on **GET STARTED**.
2. Complete the **Your Name** and **Project Title** blocks.
3. Click on **Start**.
4. Click on **Timeline to add items**, as it reads on the pop-up window that appears.
5. Complete the **Label**, **Short Description**, and **Full Description** blocks.
6. Click on the tick and drag-and-drop the item that we have just inserted, in the desired place.
7. Repeat steps 5 to 7, as many times as events you want to add.
8. When you finish the timeline, click on **Finish**.

9. When the timeline is ready, click on **Save Final**, as shown in the following screenshot:

10. Write a name for the file and click on **Save**.

11. Click on **Ok**.

How it works...

We have already designed a timeline using a website. We have done it using names of events relevant to what this famous person has achieved throughout his\her life. Thus, students have to write an essay using the information in this timeline.

We need to upload the file that we have created in our Moodle course. It means that we need to upload the timeline that we saved as PDF. So, these are the steps that you have to follow to design this activity:

1. Click on **Add an activity or resource** | **File** | **Add**.

2. Complete the **Name** and **Description** blocks.

3. In the **Content** section, click on **Add** | **Upload a file** and look for the file to upload. Then, click on **Open** | **Upload this file**.

4. Click on **Options**, and choose **Embed** within **Display**.

5. Click on **Save and display**, the file shows as shown in the following screenshot:

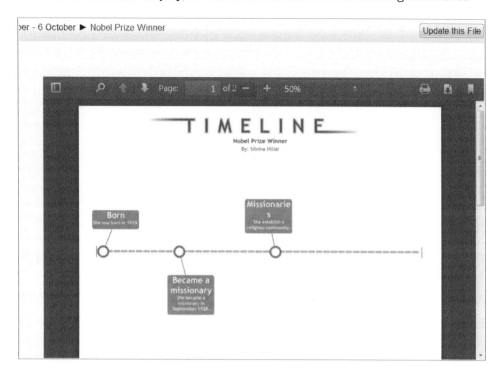

We can create another activity out of this resource for students to write their own version of the Nobel Prize winner's biography. Another option is that they upload a timeline.

By the way, the name of the Nobel Prize winner is Mother Teresa.

Creating storyboards

In this activity, we will design a storyboard using an interactive website. We will navigate to http://storybird.com/ and design a book to share with our students. It can be an original book changed to become a funny one, or telling the story in a different way, switching between good and bad, why not? Let's get ready.

Getting ready

We have to think what to write because this website allows us to write either poetry or stories, so we can copy a poem written by a well-known person and add some images to work with students. We can also ask students to design their homework using this tool. There happens to be plenty of possibilities through usage of such an amazing tool.

How to do it...

In this recipe, we will design a story for our students to read. This recipe is devoted to little children; we can also adjust it for adolescents using another type of story, but visual aids are to be different. So, let's go back to our childhood for a little!

Before designing our story, we need to sign up. There are two ways to do it, we can sign up for free, or there happens to be a paid account, which offers more possibilities to work out with stories. In this recipe, we'll use the free account. These are the steps that you have to follow:

1. Go to `http://storybird.com/` and click on **Sign up for Free** on the top-right corner.

2. Within **Account type**, select on **Teacher/Class**.

3. Complete the necessary blocks in order to create an account. Read the terms and tick the box after reading them all.

4. Click on **Create Account**, as shown in the following screenshot:

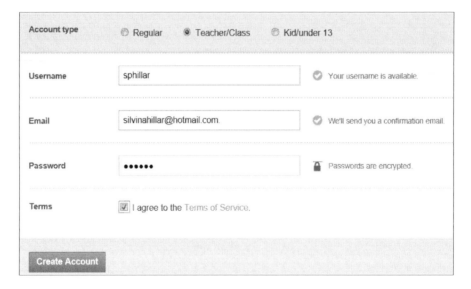

5. After receiving an e-mail confirming the account, you can start and create your story. Return to the website again and click on **You**.

6. Click on **Create**.

7. Within the search block write `ant` (or the drawing that you want to find), as shown in the following screenshot:

8. There appears a list of stories created using the said word, but we will click on **Artwork**, on the left-hand margin to look for images of the said word. There are seven artworks of the said word, in this case, as shown in the following screenshot:

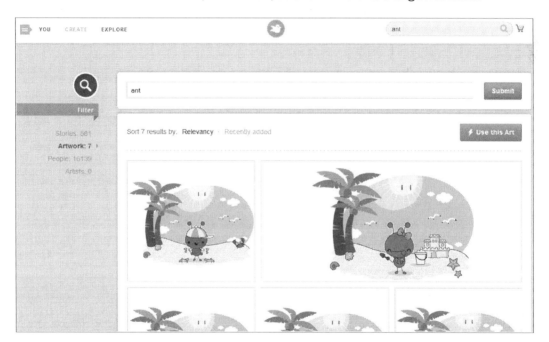

9. Click on the image that you want to choose. Click on **Use this Art** | **For a Story**, as shown in the following screenshot:

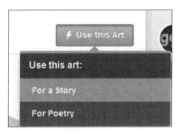

10. Click on **Cover** and start writing the story underneath the drawing. There appears circles with information on how to go on with the writing of the story.

11. Click on the type of cover and customize it. Beware that some covers are available in paid accounts only!

12. Write the title of the story and the author and click on **Save**.

13. Click on **add page** in order to add pages to the story. Drag-and-drop the images that appear on both sides of the blank page in order to create the story, as shown in the following screenshot:

14. Repeat the previous step as many times as pages you want to insert.

How it works...

When the story is ready, we have to follow some steps to get the shared link in order to share our story with students. If we happen to have a paid account, there are other ways that we can share it, such as embedding code or famous networks, but here it is not the case. So, we will follow these steps in order to get the URL:

1. When the story is ready, click on **Menu | Publish**.

2. Complete the necessary blocks and click on **Publish**.

3. Click on **Share** and copy the URL, as shown in the following screenshot:

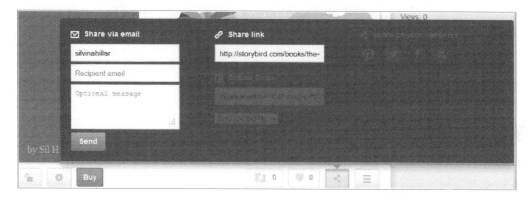

Embedding the story in Moodle

Stories are a nice asset to work within the teaching process; so students will be very happy, as well as attracted to it when we present such a resource in our Moodle course. As we have already mentioned in the previous recipe, we share the story adding a resource in our Moodle course. So, let's get ready!

Getting ready

In this recipe, we do not have to follow so many steps. We just need to upload all the work that we have done in the previous one. It is time to have our story in the Moodle course for our students to enjoy reading it.

How to do it...

We choose the weekly outline section where we want to upload the story. In this case, we are going to add a resource because we embed the URL that we had already copied in the previous recipe. Follow these steps in order to carry it out:

1. Click on **Add an activity or resource | URL**, as shown in the following screenshot:

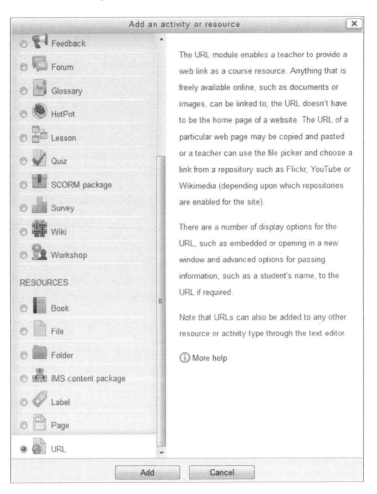

2. Click on **Add**.
3. Complete the **Name** and **Description** blocks.
4. Paste the URL of the story in the **External URL** block within **Content**.
5. Click on the drop-down menu next to **Display** and choose **Embed** within options.
6. Click on **Save and return to course**.

How it works...

When students click on the resource to read the story, they see it embedded in our Moodle course. When they hover the mouse over the sideways arrows, they go to the next or previous page. So, they see the story, as shown in the following screenshot:

Embedding the Fakebook of William Shakespeare

We have already written a story in the previous recipe, but in this one what we have to deal with is one of the most famous writers of all time. He is a man of achievement because we still read his works. So, there is a beautiful website full of resources where we can find Fakebook (it is an imitation of the famous social network) of famous people that can be embedded. Let's get ready!

Getting ready

We need to go to `http://www.classtools.net/` in order to look for the Fakebook of William Shakespeare. There are plenty of Fakebooks of famous people, such as history characters, which can also be added in your Moodle course, it will depend on which subject you are teaching. Enter the aforementioned website and start enjoying!

How to do it...

We have to follow some steps in order to look for the Fakebook of Shakespeare, but in this case we do not have to enter our Facebook account! Follow these steps to get the HTML code in order to embed it in our Moodle course:

1. Go to `http://www.classtools.net/`.

2. Click on **Fakebook** on the right-hand margin, as shown in the following screenshot:

3. You can edit the Fakebook account or you can search in the gallery; in this case go to `http://www.classtools.net/main_area/fakebook/gallery/`, as shown in the following screenshot:

4. There are many options, either real characters or even book characters. Click on the upper ribbon and choose **Literature and Language**.

5. Look for the desired character to work with, in this case William Shakespeare. When hovering the mouse over the question mark of each character, there appears a brief bio, as shown in the following screenshot:

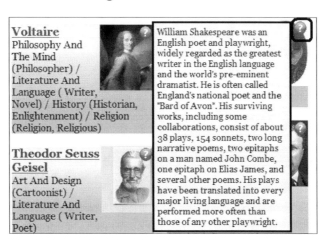

6. Click on the character to insert, in this case William Shakespeare.

7. On the right-hand margin, click on **Embed**; you can choose **Static** (Fakebook appears) or **Animation Mode** (there appear, the new posts of Shakespeare, they move).

8. Click on one of them and copy the HTML code, as shown in the following screenshot:

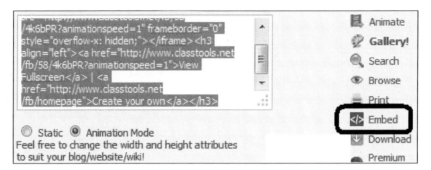

How it works...

We need to add this resource into our Moodle course. We can add a page or we can design any type of activity and use this resource as an icebreaker or so. Thus, we enter our Moodle course and choose the weekly outline section where we want to add it, and follow these steps:

1. Click on **Add an activity or resource**.

2. Click on **Page | Add**.

3. Complete the **Name** and **Description** blocks.

4. Complete the **Description** block within **Content**. Click on **Edit HTML source** and paste the code copied from the Fakebook of William Shakespeare.

5. Click on **Update**.

6. Click on **Save and display**, the activity looks as shown in the following screenshot:

2
Working with 2D and 3D Maps

In this chapter, we will cover the following recipes:

- ▶ Using maps with sceneries
- ▶ Drawing regions within a map
- ▶ Using weather maps
- ▶ Using Google Maps to locate European bridges
- ▶ Working with Yahoo! Maps
- ▶ Watching stars through Bing Maps 3D
- ▶ Drawing 3D maps using 3DVIA Shape for Maps
- ▶ Working with constellation maps
- ▶ Embedding a map of Mars
- ▶ Labeling the moon
- ▶ Watching the universe

Introduction

This chapter explains how to create and embed different types of maps, either 2D or 3D, in our Moodle courses. The maps can be interactive or static. We will use resources available in Web 2.0, as well as free and open source software. Thanks to these amazing tools, we can design and display interactive maps in our Moodle courses.

Whenever you think of a map, you may either think of the traditional planisphere or the terrestrial globe. There are several types of maps apart from the ones previously mentioned. We can work with maps of the moon, Mars, constellations, and even the universe! Thus, we are not only going to focus on our planet, we are going to travel even further!

Taking into account that this book covers the topic of general knowledge, the topic of this chapter will deal with *Traveling Around the World and Watching the Universe*. After reading this chapter, you can focus on your next holiday!

Thinking of a holiday, we can also work with weather maps, because we would need to get our clothes! So, working with weather maps would be a nice element to add to our Moodle course, not only for a Geography teacher, but also for an English teacher who would like to create a writing activity taking into account the weather.

We will also explain how to work with different types of maps and be as creative as possible. We should try to work with maps in a way that is not the standard one. That is to say, the idea is to use a map for a Geography class, but we can use maps as a resource for any type of activity, as was previously mentioned. We can also design a map for a Mathematics class thinking of statistics around the world. Another option is to work with the Geography teacher and he/she could work on another geographical feature of the place that we are working with. Therefore, in that way, we are adding more information to the place that we are exploring.

Maps are very attractive and they may become quite appealing to our students as long as we find the way to develop a rich activity by using them. We should encourage the use of maps and the available resources that we have on the Web so that students can insert them in their homework by themselves. Thus, we can develop the activities in such a way that we can either provide the map or ask them to design a map.

We can also work with maps in the case of Literature. We can ask students to draw a map of a place that has never existed in the real world, though it did in a story, thus, coming up with another bit of homework that could prove useful for students to design and carry out the map of such a place using the tools that we are going to explore in the following recipes. An example of this could be to draw the map of the country Ruritania and locate the cities of Zenda and Strealsau. These places do not exist in the real world but they exist in the book *The Prisoner of Zenda* by *Anthony Hope*. So, many things can be done out of maps!

Using maps with sceneries

In this recipe, we are going to work with an already designed map for education showing information, videos, photography, and 3D models. "The World Wonders Project is a valuable resource for students and scholars who can now virtually discover some of the most famous sites on earth. The project offers an innovative way to teach ..." This is what we read when we enter the **Education** option of this amazing website!

Getting ready

Go to http://www.google.com/culturalinstitute/worldwonders/ and find the resources mentioned before. We can choose different places of the world to work with, or travel virtually! So, let's start working with this amazing resource.

How to do it...

Think of a place in the world to explore, or we can look for a part of the world to work with. When we enter the aforementioned website, there is an image of a place and beneath there appears the map with the location of the said place. Follow these steps in order to get the URL to embed in the Moodle course:

1. Go to http://www.google.com/culturalinstitute/worldwonders/.

2. Hover the mouse pointer over the **Find by location** menu.

3. Click on **Antarctica | Cape Evans | Scott's Hut and the Explorer's Heritage...**, as shown in the following screenshot:

4. Another option is to click on the downward arrow within **Browse by themes** and choose the desired theme.

5. You choose the place to work with, in this case **Scott's Hut and the Explorers' Heritage of Antarctica**, and it has the resources shown in the following screenshot:

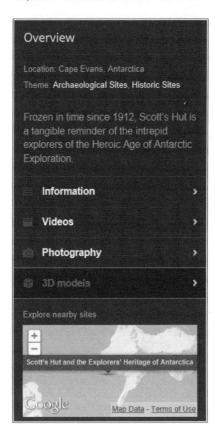

6. Click on each resource type and read the data. Click on **3D models** and you may need to install the Google Earth plugin, as shown in the following screenshot:

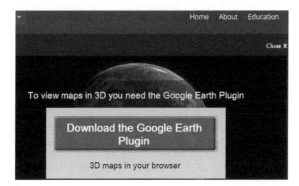

7. Install the plugin and explore the 3D model.

8. Copy the URL.

How it works...

We have already found a resource to embed in our Moodle course. There is not a possibility to get the HTML code, but we can embed it using the URL. So, we enter our Moodle course and we add this amazing resource. Follow these steps:

1. Click on **Add an activity or resource | URL | Add**.

2. Complete the **Name** and **Description** blocks.

3. Paste the URL in the **External URL** block in the **Content** section.

4. Click on the drop-down menu next to **Display** and choose **Embed**, as shown in the following screenshot:

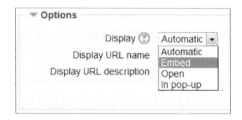

5. Click on **Save and return to course**.

Drawing regions within a map

In this recipe, we will work with Google Maps. Go to `https://maps.google.com/` to start getting ready for the recipe. There are plenty of items in this website that allow us to enrich our map, so we can enhance it by adding interesting ingredients to the recipe. We can draw a region using a polygon and change its color. We will not focus on geographical features; however, you can add this ingredient yourself when designing the activity.

Getting ready

We need a map to work with, so we have to think of a place. We can choose a country or a continent. We have to bear in mind which regions to mark. In this case, we choose a map of the world and highlight some regions. You can modify it and work with different regions within a continent or a country.

Before working with Google Maps we need to create a Google user account. You can do it from `https://accounts.google.com/SignUp` if you do not have one, because you will need it to sign in.

How to do it...

Taking into account that the topic of this chapter deals with traveling, we will draw polygons and add some comments to the said regions. Within the comments we will ask our students to choose where they would like to go, the weather, and so on. We open our default web browser and navigate to `https://mapsengine.google.com/map/`. Then, follow these steps:

1. Click on **New map**, as shown in the following screenshot:

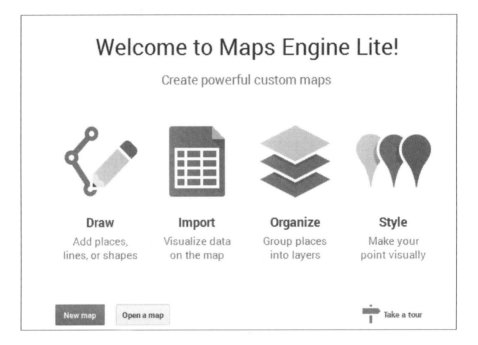

2. Zoom the map out, so that the whole world fits the screen.

3. Click on **Untitled map**. Edit the map title and description in the pop-up window that appears and click on **Save**.

4. Click on the **Add line or shape** icon and start drawing polygons in your map, as shown in the following screenshot:

5. Complete the polygon description in the pop-up window that appears when you finish drawing.

6. Draw lines showing students that they can travel from one place to another.

7. Complete the line description in the pop-up window that appears when you finish the line.

8. Click on the **Share** button.

9. Change the visibility option to **Anyone with the link** and copy the **Link to share** value.

10. The activity is designed within the map. When clicking over the regions and lines, there appears the descriptions. In this case, the descriptions were pasted just to show how you can design the activity. The descriptions will appear as **Destination Number 1**. This is shown in the following screenshot:

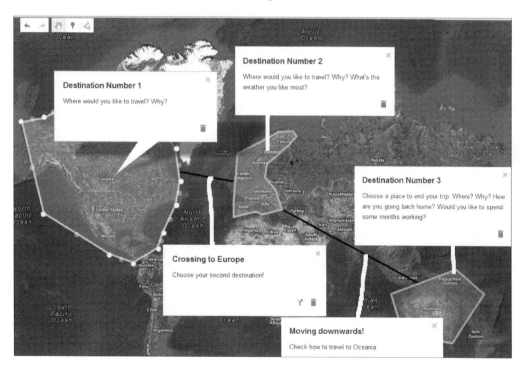

How it works...

We have already designed an activity in Google Maps, so it is time for our students to work with it. Students have to upload their submission writing a report or an article using the previous map. We need to upload it to our Moodle course. Select the weekly outline section where you want to add the activity and follow these steps:

1. Click on **Add an activity or resource | Assignment | Add**.

2. Complete the **Assignment name** and **Description** blocks.

3. Within the **Description** block, highlight a word.

4. Click on the **Insert/edit link** icon, as shown in the following screenshot:

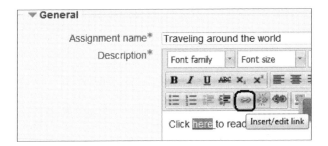

5. Complete the **Link URL** (paste the URL from Google Maps) and **Title** blocks.

6. Click on **Insert**.

7. Click on **Online text** within **Submission types**.

8. Click on **Save and display**. The activity is ready!

Using weather maps

In this recipe, we learn how to create a weather map with a click. We use the same website as in the previous recipe; it means that we use https://maps.google.com/ again. We insert the weather map as a resource, but we have to guide students on how to have the weather forecast. After that, we design activities for our students to use the map that we have just added. It is another way to use a resource, making our Moodle course more appealing to our students.

Getting ready

We can also work with small children with this resource, taking into account that they can learn weather vocabulary using maps. They can also work with the daily weather of their city. It is just a click away, zooming in or out! In this case, we are to work with the weather of the whole world!

How to do it...

Go to `https://maps.google.com/`. We can choose a place to work with. In this case, we will work with the whole world again, so we zoom out in order that all the countries fit the screen. Follow these steps:

1. Zoom out so that the world map fits the screen.

2. Hover the mouse pointer over the menu on the right-hand margin and click on **Weather**, as shown in the following screenshot:

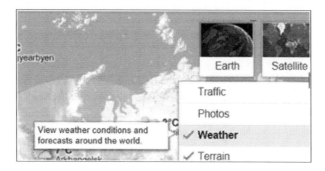

3. The weather conditions and forecasts around the world appear on the map.

4. On the left-hand margin there appears the weather forecast of some important cities, as shown in the following screenshot:

5. Click on **Hide clouds** on the left-hand margin, just to see the temperature on the map.

6. Click on the **Link** icon and copy the URL, as shown in the following screenshot:

How it works...

We have to insert the map in our Moodle course. In this case, we are going to add a resource, because we are introducing all the activities to come. So, choose where you want to insert the resource. These are the steps that you have to follow:

1. Click on **Add an activity or resource | URL | Add**.

2. Complete the **Name** and **Description** blocks.

3. Paste the URL in **External URL**.

4. Click on the drop-down menu next to **Display** and select **In pop-up**, as shown in the following screenshot:

5. Click on **Save and display**. When you click on the URL, there is a pop-up window where the weather map appears.

Using Google Maps to locate European bridges

In this recipe, we have the possibility to travel to France and visit the river Seine. There are a lot of bridges along this river, therefore we ask our students to go along this river by boat. They have to find all the bridges along it and mark them in the map. Another possibility is for us to do this task the other way round and ask them to find some information.

Getting ready

We look for a website giving information about the bridges on the Seine river, such as `http://www.pariswater.com/ponts/`. In this website, we can find the bridges on the left, and as you click on each of them, a bigger picture is displayed in the middle of the page. There is information about the bridge both in English and French.

How to do it...

We will work with maps because we have to travel through this beautiful river by boat. Our students will have to locate all the bridges along the Seine river. Therefore, we work with `http://maps.google.com/`. We open our default web browser and Google Maps website. Follow these steps in order to get the link of the map to work with:

1. Type `Seine, Paris, France` (for instance) in the search location field.

2. After you find the desired location, click on the **Link** icon, as shown in the following screenshot:

3. Copy the HTML code to paste it in the Moodle course.

How it works...

We have the map and the website with the information about the bridges. So, now we can design the resource in our Moodle course. We can add a resource, we can choose a page, and then we can add an activity. Choose where you want to insert the resource and follow these steps:

1. Click on **Add an activity or resource | Page | Add**.

2. Complete the **Name** and **Description** blocks.

3. Complete the **Page content** block within **Content**.

4. Write `Seine River`, highlight the words and click on the **Insert/edit link** icon.

5. Paste the website `http://www.pariswater.com/ponts/` in the **Link URL** block.

6. Click on the **Target** drop-down menu and choose **Open in new window (_blank)**.

7. Click on **Insert**.

8. Click on the **Edit HTML source** icon.

9. Copy-and-paste the HTML code.

10. Click on **Save and display**. The activity looks as shown in the following screenshot:

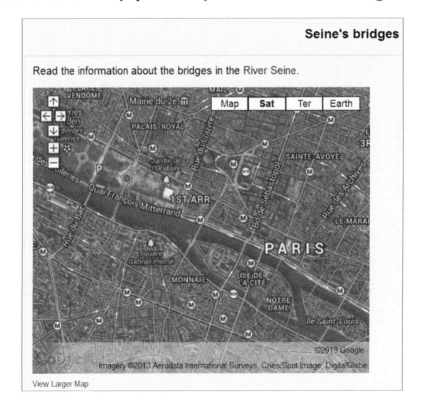

Working with Yahoo! Maps

This is a very simple recipe, just to present another resource that we can use to work with maps. It is `http://maps.yahoo.com`. Here, we will navigate to the said website and share the map using the URL.

Getting ready

We can add this map in any activity or resource within our Moodle course using the URL, so that we can link to the said website. It is another option for working with maps.

How to do it...

We have to open our default web browser and go to `http://maps.yahoo.com/`. Google Maps has more options to work with than Yahoo! Maps, but the second one is interesting as well. Zoom out the map so that the entire world fits the screen. Follow these steps in order to get the URL:

1. After getting the desired zoom, click on the **Share** icon, as shown in the following screenshot:

2. Copy the HTML code to embed it in the website.

How it works...

We have already copied the link to paste in our Moodle course. So, we now choose the section where we want to add the activity; these are the steps that you have to follow:

1. Click on **Add an activity or resource | Page | Add**.

2. Complete the **Name** and **Description** blocks.

3. Complete the **Page content** block.

4. Click on the **Edit HTML source** icon.

5. Paste the HTML code that was copied from Yahoo! Maps and click on **Update**.

6. Click on **Save and display**; the activity looks as shown in the following screenshot:

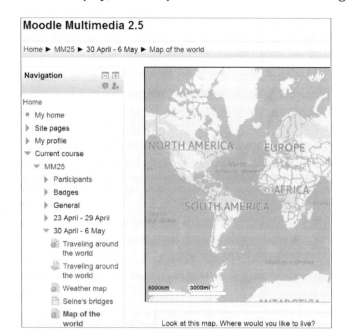

Watching stars through Bing Maps 3D

In this activity, we will travel even further, to the universe. We can see the part of the universe in some clicks. There are many apps to explore and they'll take a whole book about them, so in this recipe we will just explore watching the stars, but we can do much more with Bing Maps.

Getting ready

We have to design either a resource or an activity about watching the stars, so in this recipe we add a resource in our Moodle course because we want students to explore them, taking their time. After this amazing resource we can add an activity with homework for them to complete.

How to do it...

We have to open our default web browser and then go to `http://www.bing.com/maps/`. Then, we have to follow these steps to be able to watch the stars:

1. Zoom out the map so that the whole world fits the screen.

2. Next to **EXPLORE MAP APPS**, on the left hand side margin, click on **see all**, as shown in the following screenshot:

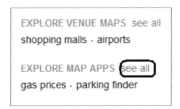

3. There appears a pop-up window with apps; click on the **WorldWide Telescope** icon, as shown in the following screenshot:

4. On the left-hand margin there appears the **WorldWide Telescope** app. Click on **Start Here**.

5. Click on the desired location in the world to watch the stars. As the map is zoomed out you can choose the place where you want to watch the stars.

6. When you click, the map zooms out and you can see the stars.

7. On the left-hand margin the app has several icons that you can explore, as shown in the following screenshot:

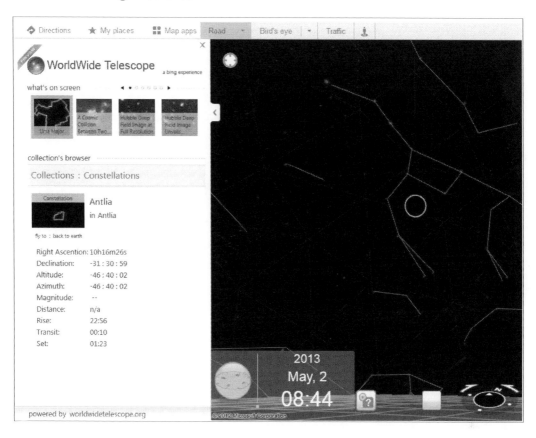

8. On the right-hand margin on the top of the screen, there appears the **Share** icon, click on it.

9. Copy the URL, which appears, as shown in the following screenshot:

How it works...

We have already created the multimedia asset to insert in our Moodle course. This part of the recipe is very simple; we add a resource in our Moodle course. These are the steps that you have to follow:

1. Click on **Add an activity or resource | URL | Add**.

2. Complete the **Name** and **Description** blocks.

3. Complete the **External URL** block and paste the link copied from Bing Maps.

4. Click on **Options**.

5. Click on the drop-down menu next to **Display** and choose **Embed**.

6. Click on **Save and display**; the activity looks as shown in the following screenshot:

Drawing 3D maps using 3DVIA Shape for Maps

This activity is very appealing because we can draw in a map. Therefore, we select a city and either design a task for our students to draw in the map or draw in the map and ask our students their opinion. In this recipe, we do the latter. We need a Windows Live account in order to publish the model that we create afterwards. Unfortunately, this activity is limited to Windows users.

Getting ready

Open `http://www.3dvia.com/products/3dvia-shape-for-maps/`. Then, click on **FREE DOWNLOAD** and follow the installation wizard in order to install the software. We can build models, such as the one shown in the following screenshot:

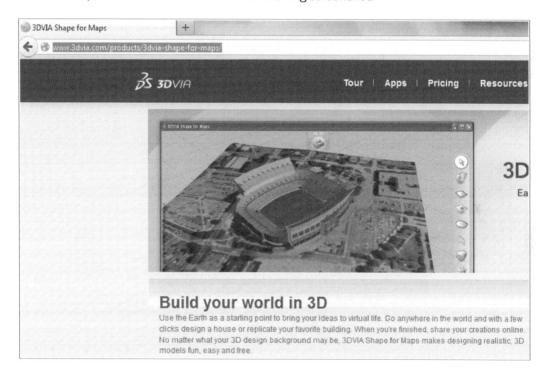

How to do it...

After downloading and installing it, an icon will appear on our desktop. Before using 3DVIA Shape for Maps, we need to install Bing! Maps 3D, otherwise we will not be able to start modeling. We need to go to `http://big-maps-3d.en.softonic.com/` and click on **Free Download**, as shown in the following screenshot:

Follow the installation wizard in order to fulfill the installation process. While installing, there appear different screenshots, they give advice about the different ways that we can use this software in order to design different types of activities. When the installation is ready, there appears an icon on your desktop.

In this activity, we ask students to travel to Cape Town, South Africa. We design a house and ask them what changes they would make to the house if they happened to go there and live for a school year. We run 3DVIA Shape for Maps, and follow these steps in order to design the activity:

1. Type the location that we want to see in the map in the block that says **Type your location here...**, as shown in the following screenshot:

2. Click on the magnifying glass icon. Click on **Road** and zoom in the map.

3. Click on **Start modeling...**. The map will appear as a background image. You are going to start modeling a house.

4. Click on the **Grid Options (G)** icon to check the orientation of the rectangle, as shown in the following screenshot:

5. Click on the **Rectangle (R)** icon and draw a rectangle. You have to click to start and click to finish, as shown in the following screenshot:

6. Click on the **Push n Pull (P)** icon to add volume to the rectangle. Move the mouse upwards.

7. Click on the **Draw (D)** icon and draw a line in the middle of the roof of the house.

8. Click on the **Deform (M)** icon. Select the line that you have just drawn and drag the yellow arrow in order to create a roof.

9. Click on the **Rectangle (R)** icon again, in order to draw the doors and the windows of the house.

10. Click on the **Rotate** icon so that you draw the back doors or windows of the house as well.

11. Click on the **Push n Pull (P)** icon to give volume to the doors and windows.

12. Click on the **Paint (X)** icon so that we can decorate the house. You can choose different textures, paints, and so on.

13. You can also add some elements to the house, such as trees, cars, and a swimming pool. Type what you want to add in the search box at the bottom.

14. Click on **Publish**. Complete the following pop-up window:

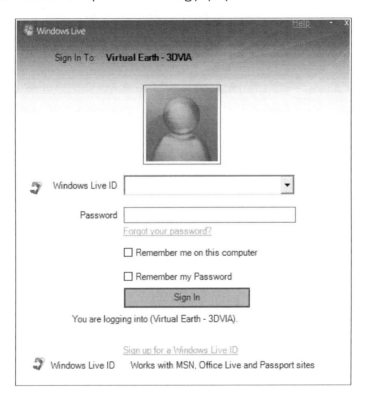

15. Another pop-up window will appear. You have to give a name for the model. Then click on **Publish**.

16. Click on **Display on map**. An icon appears in Bing Maps, as shown in the following screenshot:

17. Click on the icon.
18. Sign in to Bing Maps.
19. Click on **Save to your places**.
20. Click on the drop-down arrow, choose a place, and click on **Save**.
21. There appears a pop-up window displaying where the place has been added. Click on **Go there**, as shown in the following screenshot:

22. Click on **Share** on the right-hand margin on the top and copy the HTML code.

How it works...

We have just created the multimedia part of the activity. Now, we can create a database in which we ask our students to give their opinion about the location of the house, so we can embed the multimedia element that we have created in our Moodle course. Another option would be to create a forum activity where students can debate about this creation. We can work together with the Geography teacher, who can add data about the climate of the said place and add any other changes to the house. These are the steps that you have to follow:

1. Click on **Add an activity or resource | Database | Add**.

2. Complete the **Name** and **Description** blocks.

3. Click on the **Edit HTML source** icon. Paste the code in order to embed the map. Click on **Update**.

4. Click on **Save and display**.

5. Click on the drop-down menu in **Create a new field** and choose **Text**.

6. Complete **Field name** with a question. Click on **Add**. Write as many questions as necessary to guide students to think of possible changes to the house.

7. Repeat steps 6 and 7 to create more questions.

8. Click on **Save | Continue** and go back to the course. The activity is ready to work with!

Working with constellation maps

In this recipe, we will work with constellations. We have to design an activity for students to work with them. One activity could be to travel back in time and tell our students how sailors used to guide themselves with stars. Though we are not going to use that kind of trip or go back in time, it's just a tip for you to take into account!

Getting ready

We have just found what to use to work with constellation maps. It is time to design the activity. We are travelling, and from the window of our spaceship we can see many stars; as you know, these stars seen together from Earth form different constellations.

We will work with this map because students can travel in space and see the constellations. After they explore the universe, they complete a glossary in our Moodle course with the names of the constellations. They add the necessary information about them.

How to do it...

We can use an interesting website that allows us to embed the map of constellations. Go to `http://www.astroviewer.com/index.php` and follow these steps to get the HTML code to embed in our Moodle course:

1. Click on **For your website**.

2. There appears options to embed. Click on **current night sky**, as shown in the following screenshot:

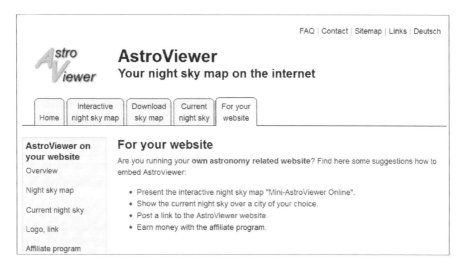

 Image credit for Mini-AstroViewer icon: `http://www.astroviewer.com`, copyright by Dirk Matussek.

3. Write the name of the city within the **generate HTML code** block.

4. Copy the code.

There appears a preview of the map beneath.

How it works...

After so much travel, students deserve to watch the constellation and play. Therefore, we add a tool where students can watch the map and play a game. Follow these steps in order to add the activity:

1. Click on **Add an activity or resource | External Tool | Add**.

2. Click on the arrow next to **General**.

3. Complete the **Activity Name** field.

4. Within the **Activity Description** block, click on the **Edit HTML source** icon and paste the HTML code.

5. Click on **Update**.

6. Tick the item **Display description on course page**, as shown in the following screenshot:

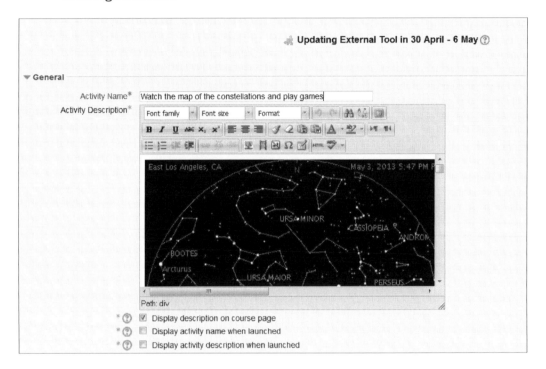

7. Complete the **Launch URL** block with the following URL:

   `http://www.kidsastronomy.com/astroskymap/constellation_hunt.htm`

8. Click on **Save and return to course**. The activity is ready to be enjoyed!

Embedding a map of Mars

In this recipe, we will focus on the Red Planet—Mars. We will work with a website that allows us to embed a map of Mars. Therefore, visit `http://hubblesite.org/gallery/album/pr1999027f/`. Apart from embedding the map, we also have the possibility of saving the image of the said map, so that we can upload it to our Moodle course.

Getting ready

We can also add more information about this planet. Therefore, we can search data for educators at `http://amazing-space.stsci.edu/eds/overviews/fastfacts/ mars.php.p=Teaching+tools%40%2Ceds%2Ctools%2C%3ESolar+system%40%2Ceds %2Ctools%2Ctopic%2Csolarsystem.php`. According to the type of activity we develop, we can choose an appropriate link.

How to do it...

We design the following activity in two parts. The first part is a resource and the second part consists of the production of our students (the result of the trip). Thus, we ask our students to travel to the Red Planet, but before doing so we have to give them information about the place to visit. Follow these steps in order to add the resource in our Moodle course:

1. Click on **Add an activity or resource | URL | Add**.
2. Complete the **Name** and **Description** blocks.
3. Complete the **External URL** block within the **Content** box. Copy the following URL:

   `http://amazing-space.stsci.edu/eds/overviews/fastfacts/mars. php.p=Teaching+tools%40%2Ceds%2Ctools%2C%3ESolar+system%40%2Ced s%2Ctools%2Ctopic%2Csolarsystem.php`

4. Click on the downward arrow next to **Options**.
5. Next to **Display**, choose **Embed**.
6. Click on **Save and return to course**. The activity looks as shown in the following screenshot:

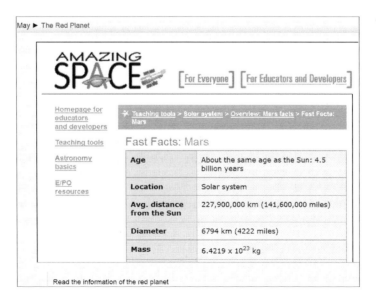

How it works...

We are going to embed the map of Mars because we do not want our students to get lost. After that, we ask them to write down their experience in their virtual journey, including as much information as possible. We can also direct the assignment by guiding them on how to produce their report.

We design the activity in **Upload a single file**. Therefore, follow these steps in order to add the assignment to our Moodle course:

1. Click on **Add an activity or resource | Assignment | Add**.

2. Complete the **Assignment name** and **Description** blocks.

3. Go to `http://hubblesite.org/gallery/album/pr1999027f/`. Click on **EMBED**, and copy the HTML code that appears.

4. Go back to the Moodle course, click on the **Edit HTML source** icon and paste the HTML code that you have copied before. Then, click on **Update**.

5. You can also adjust the assignment settings.

6. Click on **Save and return to course**. The activity looks as shown in the following screenshot:

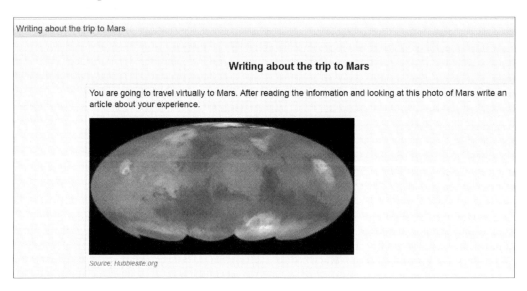

Writing about the trip to Mars

Writing about the trip to Mars

You are going to travel virtually to Mars. After reading the information and looking at this photo of Mars write an article about your experience.

Source: Hubblesite.org

Image credit: `http://hubblesite.org/gallery/album/pr1999027f/`.

Photo credit: Steve Lee (University of Colorado), Jim Bell (Cornell University), Mike Wolff (Space Science Institute), and NASA.

Labeling the moon

In this recipe, we travel to the moon. Therefore, we work with Google Earth. We can see the moon in 3D. We can download it from `http://www.google.com/earth/index.html`. Click on **Download Google Earth** and follow the installation wizard. We label the parts of the moon that we want our students to explore.

We can also embed related videos from `http://www.youtube.com`, which are available in Google Earth. It would add an extra multimedia element to our activity in order to enhance it a little bit. Besides, this recipe is even spicier.

Getting ready

Google Earth allows us to watch not only the Earth but also other planets. So, after installing it, there appears an icon on our desktop, we run it and click on the planet, and choose **Moon**, as shown in the following screenshot:

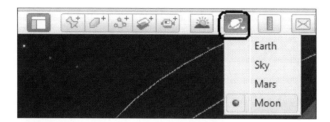

How to do it...

We choose a section of the moon that we want our students to explore. We can choose one of the **Apollo Missions** options on the left-hand margin in Google Earth within **Layers** in **Earth Gallery**. We click on **Apollo Missions** and choose **Apollo 17** because there is also an interesting video available on YouTube, which we can embed in order to strengthen our activity.

We follow these steps in order to capture a photo labeling the moon in the part that we want our students to explore. Follow these steps to work with Google Earth:

1. Click on **Apollo 17**. A pop-up window will appear displaying information about the different resources available.
2. Click on **Zoom in** at the bottom of the window in order to explore the landing site.

3. Click on the **Add placemark** icon on top. Complete the pop-up window, as shown in the following screenshot:

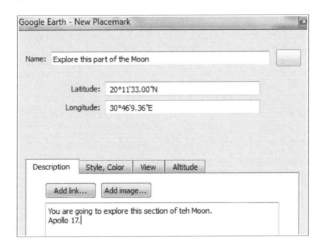

4. Click on **OK**.

5. Click on **File | Save | Save Image...**.

6. Complete the **File name** block.

7. Click on **Save**.

8. You can also choose a video about this place of the moon to embed it in our Moodle course. Click on **Apollo 17** within **Apollo Mission**.

9. A pop-up window displaying images and videos appears. Click on the video to embed in the Moodle course.

10. Click on **Watch on YouTube**, as shown in the following screenshot:

11. Click on **Share | Embed**, and copy the HTML code in order to embed the said video in our Moodle course.

How it works...

We have plenty of multimedia assets to work with. It is time to create an activity in our Moodle course about traveling to the moon. We are going to create a forum because we want our students to add their opinions about this mission. Therefore, choose the weekly outline section where you want to add the activity and follow these steps:

1. Click on **Add an activity or resource | Forum | Add**.

2. Complete the **Forum name** and **Description** blocks.

3. Click on the **Insert/edit image** icon.

4. Click on **Find or upload an image | Upload a file | Browse**.

5. Click on the image of the moon that we have saved before.

6. Click on **Open | Upload this file | Insert**.

7. Complete the **Image description** block.

8. Click on **Insert**.

9. Click on the **Edit HTML source** icon.

10. Paste the HTML code from YouTube.

11. Click on **Update**.

12. Click on **Save and return to course**. You have created a rich activity!

Watching the universe

In this recipe, we design a very simple activity. We are going to go on traveling into space and watch the universe so that we can explore other planets. Therefore, let's get ready for our last stop.

Getting ready

This time, we will explore the solar system in 3D. We have already worked with many websites that allow us to work with maps, either to embed them, take a picture of the desired location, or make a link to them. So, you are free to choose one of these websites. But in this recipe, we can explore each planet and read information about them just by clicking on them.

How to do it...

Go to `http://www.sunaeon.com/#/solarsystem/` in order to explore the solar system. Then, we go to our Moodle course and choose the weekly outline section where we want to add the activity. Follow these steps:

1. Click on **Add an activity or resource | URL | Add**.

2. Complete the **Name** and **Description** blocks.

3. Write `http://www.sunaeon.com/#/solarsystem/` within the **External URL** block.

4. Click on **Options**.

5. Click on the drop-down menu next to **Display** and choose **Embed**.

6. Click on **Save and display**. The activity looks as shown in the following screenshot:

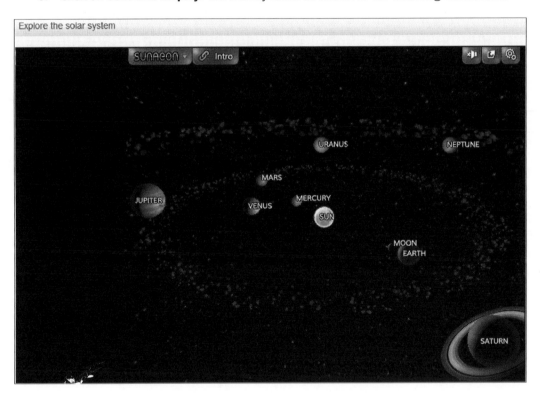

How it works...

When hovering the mouse over the planets, there appears their names. We can also explore each planet and there appears additional information that is displayed on a pop-up window. The structure of each planet is also shown.

This is a rich activity, which shows information about the planets in the Milky Way. Besides, we can work using this data for different purposes. Students do love working with planets and imagining that there might be life outside, so the activity is to think how to use these planets in our Moodle course!

3
Working with Different Types of Interactive Charts

In this chapter, we will cover the following recipes:

- ▸ Inserting column charts
- ▸ Embedding a line chart
- ▸ Designing a graph out of a choice activity
- ▸ Creating bar charts with hyperlinks
- ▸ Working with area charts
- ▸ Creating a poll and designing a surface chart
- ▸ Drawing a donut interactive chart
- ▸ Designing a map chart
- ▸ Creating a gauge chart

Introduction

This chapter explains how to create and embed 2D and 3D charts. They can also be interactive or static and we will insert them into our Moodle courses. We will mainly work with several spreadsheets in order to include diverse tools and techniques that are also present. The main idea is to display data in charts and provide students with the necessary information for their activities.

We will also work with a variety of charts and deal with statistics as a baseline topic in this chapter. We can either develop a chart or work with ready-to-use data. You can design these types of activities in your Moodle course, together with a math teacher.

When thinking of statistics, we generally have in mind a picture of a chart and some percentages representing the data of the chart. We can change that paradigm and create a different way to draw and read statistics in our Moodle course. We design charts with drawings, map charts, links to websites, and other interesting items.

We can also redesign the charts, comprising numbers, with different assets because we want not only to enrich, but also strengthen the diversity of the material for our Moodle course since some students are not keen on numbers and dislike activities with them. So, let's give another chance to statistics!

There are different types of graphics to show statistics. Therefore, we show a variety of tools available to display different results. No matter what our subject is, we can include these types of graphics in our Moodle course.

You can use these graphics to help your students give weight to their arguments and express themselves using key points clearly. We teach students to include graphics, read them, and use them as a tool of communication.

We can also work with puzzles related to statistics. That is to say, we can invent a graph and give tips or clues to our students so that they can sort out which percentages belong to the chart. In other words, we can create a listening comprehension activity, a reading comprehension activity, or a math problem. We can just upload or embed the chart, create an appealing activity, and give clues to our students so that they can think of the items belonging to the chart.

Inserting column charts

In this activity, we work with the website `http://populationaction.org/`. We work with statistics about different topics that are related to each other. We can explore different countries and use several charts in order to draw conclusions. We can also embed the charts in our Moodle course.

Getting ready

We need to think of a country to work with. We can compare statistics of population, water, croplands, and forests of different countries in order to draw conclusions about their futures.

How to do it...

We go to the website mentioned earlier and follow some steps in order to get the HTML code to embed it in our Moodle course. In this case, we choose Canada. These are the steps to follow:

1. Enter `http://populationaction.org/` in the browser window.

2. Navigate to **Publications | Data & Maps**.

3. Click on **People in the Balance**.

4. Click on the down arrow next to the **Country or Region Name** search block and choose **Canada**, as shown in the following screenshot:

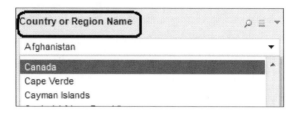

5. Go to the bottom of the page and click on **Share**.

6. Copy the HTML code, as shown in the following screenshot:

7. Click on **Done**.

How it works...

It is time to embed the charts in our Moodle course. Another option is to draw the charts using a spreadsheet. So, we choose the weekly outline section where we want to add this activity and perform the following steps:

1. Click on **Add an activity or resource**.

2. Click on **Forum | Add**.

3. Complete the **Forum name** block.

4. Click on the down arrow in **Forum type** and choose **Q and A forum**.

5. Complete the **Description** block.

6. Click on the **Edit HTML source** icon.

7. Paste the HTML code that was copied.

8. Click on **Update**.

9. Click on the down arrow next to **Subscription mode** and choose **Forced subscription**.

10. Click on **Save and display**. The activity looks as shown in the following screenshot:

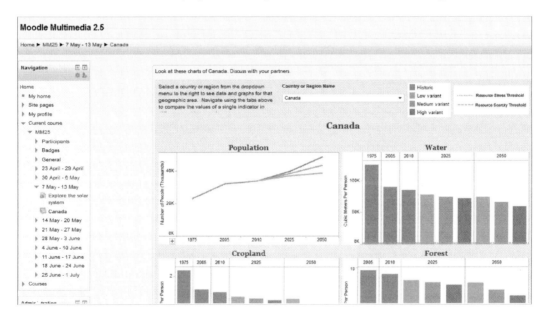

Embedding a line chart

In this recipe, we will present the estimated number of people (in millions) using a particular language over the Internet. To do this, we may include images in our spreadsheet in accordance with the method being used to design the activity. Instead of writing the name of the languages, we insert the flags that represent the language used. We design the line chart taking into account the statistical operations carried out at `http://www.internetworldstats.com/stats7.htm`.

Getting ready

We carry out the activity using **Google Docs**. We have to sign in and follow the steps required to design a spreadsheet file. We have several options for working with the document. After you have an account to work with Google Drive, let's see how to make our line chart!

How to do it...

We work with s spreadsheet because we need to make calculations and create a chart. First, we need to create a document in the spreadsheet. Therefore, we need to perform the following steps:

1. Click on **Create | Spreadsheet**, as shown in the following screenshot:

2. Write the name of the languages spoken in the **A** column.

3. Write the figures in the **B** column (from the `http://www.internetworldstats.com/stats7.htm` website).

4. Select the data from **A1** up to the **B11** column. Click on **Insert | Chart**.

5. Edit your chart using the **Chart Editor**, as shown in the following screenshot:

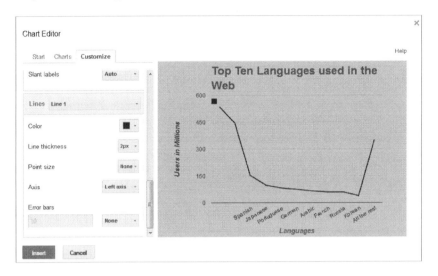

6. Click on **Insert**.

7. Add the images of the flags corresponding to the languages spoken. Position the cursor over **C1** and click on **Insert | Image....**

8. Another pop-up window will appear. You have several ways to upload images, as shown in the following screenshot:

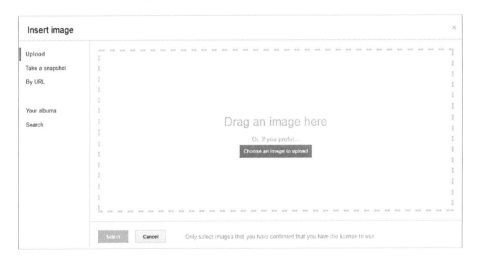

9. Click on **Choose an image to upload** and insert the image from your computer.

10. Click on **Select**.

11. Repeat the same process for all the languages. Steps 7 to 11 are optional.

12. Click on the chart.

13. Click on the down arrow in **Share | Publish chart...**, as shown in the following screenshot:

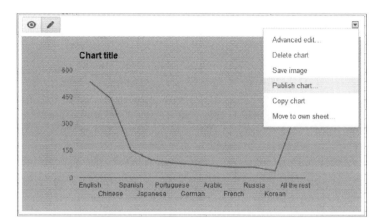

14. Click on the down arrow next to **Select a public format** and choose **Image**, as shown in the following screenshot:

15. Copy the HTML code that appears, as shown in the previous screenshot.

16. Click on **Done**.

How it works...

We have just designed the chart that we want our students to work with. We are going to embed the chart in our Moodle course; another option is to share the spreadsheet and allow students to draw the chart. If you want to design a warm-up activity for students to guess or find out which the top languages used over the Internet are, you could add a chat, forum, or a question in the course.

In this recipe, we are going to create a wiki so that students can work together. So, select the weekly outline section where you want to add the activity and perform the following steps:

1. Click on **Add an activity or resource**.
2. Click on **Wiki | Add**.
3. Complete the **Wiki name** and **Description** blocks.
4. Click on the **Edit HTML source** icon and paste the HTML code that we have previously copied. Then click on **Update**.
5. Complete the **First page name** block.
6. Click on **Save and return to course**. The activity looks as shown in the following screenshot:

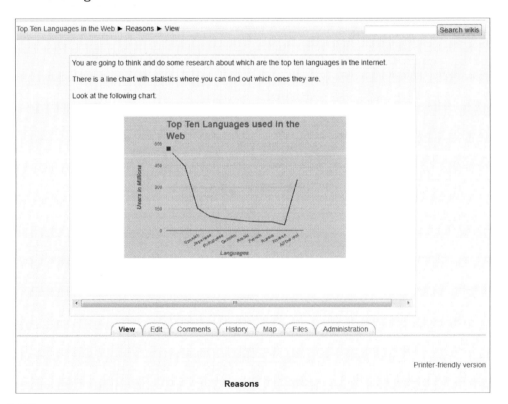

Designing a graph out of a choice activity

In this recipe, we design a choice activity in Moodle and, after creating the choices, Moodle creates a graph. This graph is to be created after making a survey with our students' participation. Therefore, our first step is to design a survey in our Moodle course.

How to do it...

We design an activity to ask our students to vote in order to create the chart. We create the activity as a choice so that students can choose their favorite type of computer games. Afterwards, the chart shows the results.

Choose the weekly outline section where you want to add the activity. The following are the steps that you are going to take:

1. Click on **Add an activity or resource**.
2. Click on **Choice | Add**.
3. Complete the **Choice name** and **Description** blocks.
4. Complete the **Options** block.
5. Complete the **Restrict answering to this time period**, **Miscellaneous settings**, and **Common module settings** blocks, as shown in the following screenshot:

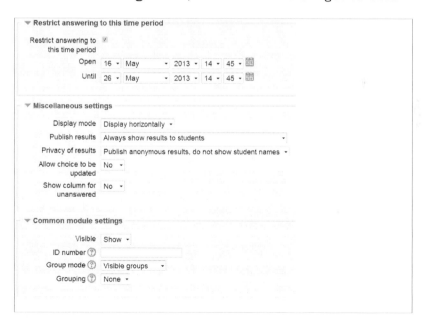

6. Click on **Save and return to course**.

How it works...

Students must click on the activity and vote. The way that this activity was designed, it won't allow students to vote more than once, therefore the activity works, as shown in the following screenshot:

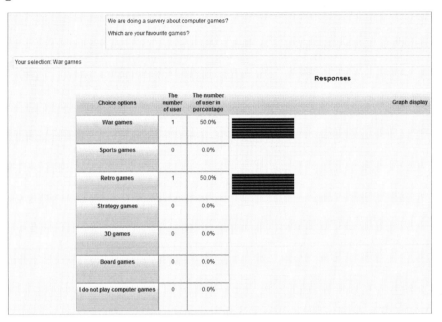

Creating bar charts with hyperlinks

In this recipe, we perform a very simple activity. We use an OpenOffice spreadsheet, if you do not happen to have it you can download it from the website `http://www.openoffice.org/download/`.

Another option happens to be Microsoft Excel. You can download a free trial version from the website `http://office.microsoft.com/en-us/try/try-office-2010-FX101868838.aspx?WT%2Emc%5Fid=MSCOM%5Fbnr%5Fenus%5Ftry`.

Getting ready

We will design a database activity in our Moodle course to survey students on the sports they play. We'll just carry out simple statistics; we are not focusing on other factors, though a math teacher can help us. We'll design this activity in two parts: the first part is the survey of our students and the second part consists of gathering the data and designing a chart using an OpenOffice spreadsheet, creating the hyperlinks through a website, and uploading it to our Moodle course.

How to do it...

We enter our Moodle course and design the database activity for gathering information about the sports students play. Select the weekly outline section and follow these steps in order to develop the activity:

1. Click on **Add an activity or resource**.
2. Click on **Database | Add**.
3. Complete the **Name** and **Description** blocks.
4. Click on **Save and display**.
5. Click on the down arrow in **Create a new field** and choose **Textarea**, as shown in the following screenshot:

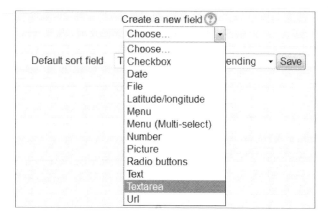

6. Fill in the **Textarea** fields with categories of sports which our students are likely to play.
7. Click on **Add**.
8. Repeat steps 5-7 as many times as required.

9. Go back to the course. The activity looks as shown in the following screenshot:

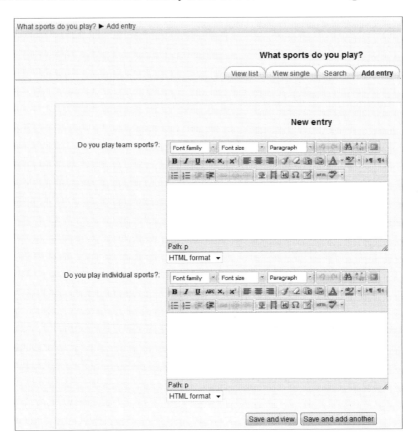

How it works...

We have just designed the survey to be carried out in our class. Now, it is time to design the bar chart to insert into our Moodle course telling the rest of the class which sports their friends play. We are going to work with an OpenOffice spreadsheet; follow these steps so that you can design the activity:

1. Complete the spreadsheet using the information that you obtain from the database activity from the Moodle course after students have completed the activity.

2. Select the first group of columns with the figures, click on **Insert | Chart**, and choose a graph.

3. The chart appears and you may edit the chart.

4. Click on **File | Save As...**.Write a name for the file and click on **Save**. The file may look as shown in the following screenshot:

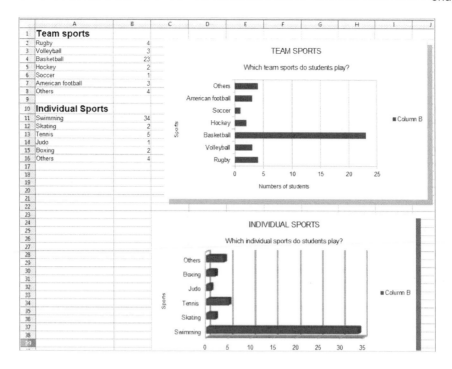

There's more...

We can insert hyperlinks in the chart that we have just created, though we must use another website because it isn't possible to do this in the OpenOffice spreadsheet. Therefore, we click on the graph, right-click on it, and click on **Copy**, as shown in the following screenshot:

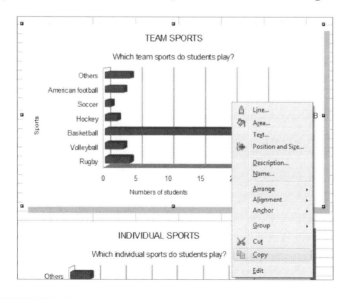

Paste the image in either Paint or Inkscape (simple graphics software). Repeat the same process for the other chart.

Inserting hyperlinks into the images

We have just saved the charts as images. Therefore, we can add hyperlinks to those images. We can do it using a web page, although there happens to be other options as well. Visit `http://www.image-maps.com/` and perform the following steps in order to get the hyperlinks:

1. Click on **Browse...**, choose the image that you want to upload, and click on **Open**.

2. Click on **Start Mapping Your Image**s as shown in the following screenshot:

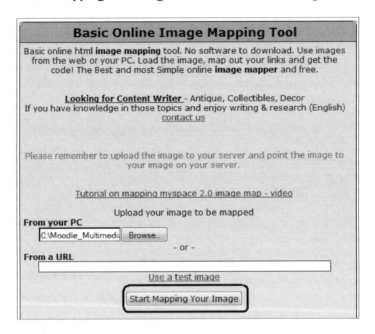

3. Click on **continue to next step**.

4. Click on **Rectangle**. Drag-and-drop the rectangle that appears and form its shape such that it covers the size of the bar in the chart.

5. Complete the **Link for this map** and **Title/Alt for this map** blocks.

6. Click on **Save**.

7. Repeat steps 4-6 for each bar. When you finish adding the hyperlinks, click on **Get Your Code**.

8. Click on **HTML Code**.

9. Select the code and copy it, as shown in the following screenshot:

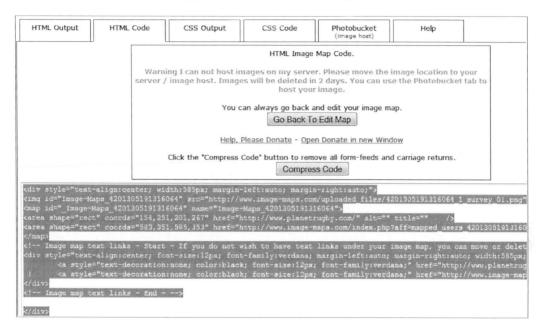

10. Copy the code.

11. Enter the Moodle course and create an activity for students to draw conclusions about sports played in the class.

12. Paste the code which will display the chart with the hyperlinks. You also have to upload the image file in the Moodle course.

13. You need to edit the name of the image file in the HTML code so that the image in the HTML code and the image that you've uploaded in the Moodle course have the same name.

14. The following is an example of an assignment activity. When hovering the mouse over the bar, a hyperlink is displayed at the bottom, as shown in the following screenshot:

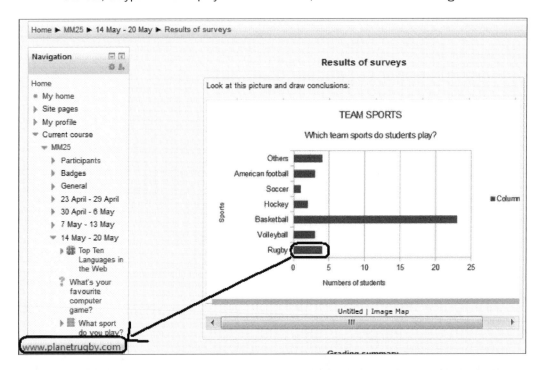

Working with area charts

We design this activity using the website `http://sheet.zoho.com/login.do?serviceurl=/home.do`. First of all, you have to sign up for free and then we can design our chart there. It is very interesting because we have access to it anywhere. Besides, we can also embed it in our Moodle course!

Getting ready

We are not going to survey our students. We can look for online statistics about any topic or we can upload an existing file to the previously mentioned website. Therefore, we upload the previous activity that we designed in OpenOffice to `http://sheet.zoho.com/`.

Considering the fact that we are working with area charts, we can add another element to the survey; we can add figures that show which sports students played last year. We have to find comparisons between them in order to design an area chart depicting the statistics.

How to do it...

We have to sign up before we can create the activity. After you sign in, the steps that you have to follow in order to design the activity are as follows:

1. Click on **Home** in your Zoho account.

2. Click on **Docs** near the right-hand margin, as shown in the following screenshot:

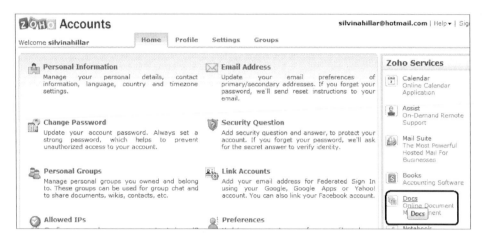

3. Click on **Create | Spreadsheet**.

4. Navigate to **File | Import | Browse**. Click on the file that you want to upload by clicking on **Open**. Finally, click on **Import**, as shown in the following screenshot:

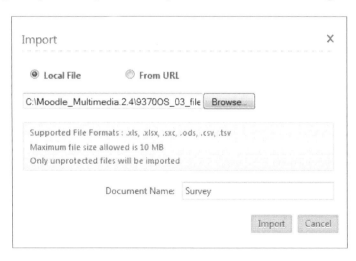

5. Click on **Close**.

6. The file created resides within our files on Zoho.

7. Click on **File** | **Open**. Click on the file that we have just imported.

8. Add data in another column; show the new figures (from this year) in **C**.

9. Click on the chart because the figures were also imported.

10. Navigate to **Edit** | **Chart type** | **Area Chart**. Click on **OK**, as shown in the following screenshot:

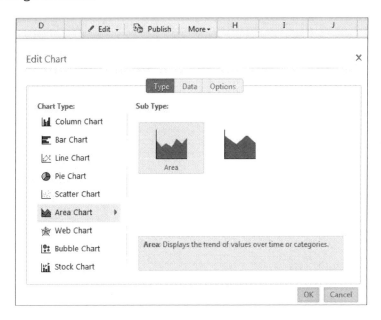

11. Click on **Data**, add the newly created column **C**, and click on **OK**.

12. Click on the down arrow next to **Share**. Under **Publish**, the **Allow to export** block is ticked, as shown in the following screenshot:

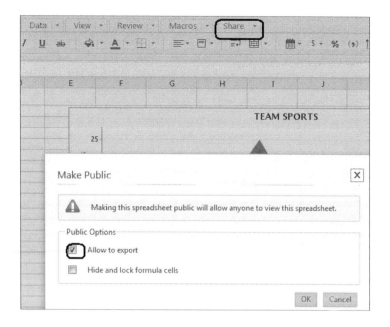

13. Click on **OK**.

14. Click on **Share | Embed** within the ribbon. Copy the HTML code, as shown in the following screenshot:

15. Click on **Close**.

16. Save the file.

How it works...

We did not create a chart in this activity because the idea was that you would learn how to use an existing one and import it to another online spreadsheet. It is time to embed this area chart in our Moodle course. So, we can add, as a database, a third element to the activity that we first designed. We are going to create a chat activity so that there is interaction among our students and they can talk about what their free-time activities are. Perform the following steps:

1. Click on **Add an activity or resource**.
2. Click on **Chat | Add**.
3. Complete the **Name of this chat room** and **Description** fields.
4. Click on the **Edit HTML source** icon and paste the HTML code of the spreadsheet.
5. Click on **Save and display**. The activity looks as shown in the following screenshot:

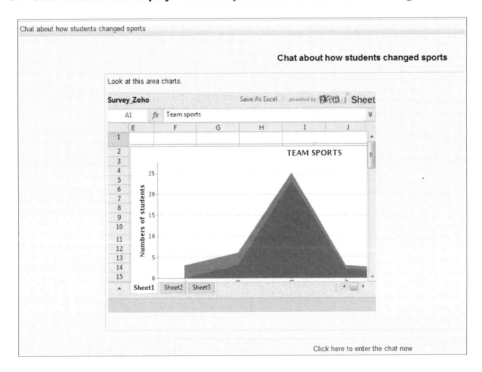

Creating a poll and designing a surface chart

We are going to create another poll in our Moodle course. In previous recipes, we have already created a poll; but, this time, we'll design it using **Feedback**. We ask students and they have to provide their answers. Let's get ready!

Getting ready

We will design the poll using Feedback within activities and create the chart drawing by exporting the file from Moodle; Feedback has this advantage. The poll has to do with Music. The question is: Which device do you use to listen to music?

How to do it...

We enter our Moodle course, choose the weekly outline section where we want to place the activity, and perform the following steps in order to carry out the activity:

1. Click on **Add an activity or resource**.
2. Click on **Feedback | Add**.
3. Complete the **Name** and **Description** blocks.
4. Click on **Save and display**.
5. Click on **Edit questions** in the top menu.
6. Click on the down arrow within the **Add question to activity** block and select **Short text answer**, as shown in the following screenshot:

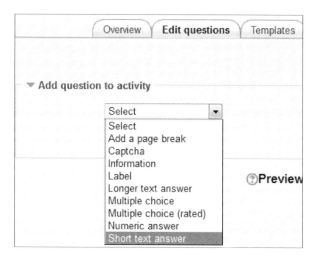

7. Write the question Which device do you use to listen to music? in the **Question** block.
8. Click on **Save question**.
9. Go back to the course.

How it works...

Students will answer the poll only once. We can see the answers of the poll and export the files to OpenOffice or Microsoft Excel and draw a chart using them without typing the data. Feedback generates an `.xls` file; this file can be opened with either Microsoft Excel or an OpenOffice spreadsheet, depending on which one is used on your computer. Perform the following steps in order to draw the surface chart:

1. Click on **Analysis | Export to Excel** (or OpenOffice, depending on the software you use).

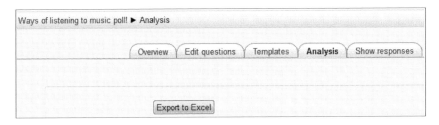

2. A pop-up window will appear displaying a message to open/save the file, click on **OK** for any of the files listed.

3. Save the file.

4. Highlight the necessary data to draw a surface chart. Navigate to **Insert | Other Charts | Surface** (you may also use another type of chart, such as bars).

5. The chart may look as shown in the following screenshot:

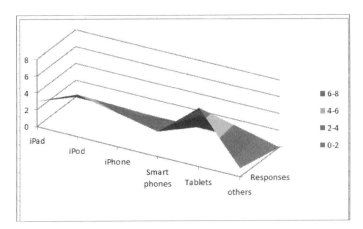

6. Right-click on the chart and select **Copy**. Paste the chart in Paint or Inkscape and save the file as `.png`. In this case, you can upload the image of the chart to the Moodle course and design another activity showing the students the result of the poll.

It appears on both screenshots in this recipe in Microsoft Excel, though it is also possible to do it in an OpenOffice spreadsheet if that happens to be the software that you use.

Drawing a donut interactive chart

We are going to create an interactive chart using OpenOffice Draw. We can insert a chart in a very simple way. We can also add images to the chart and hyperlinks to the images; we can design the same type of activity, saving the image as `.png`, and use `http://www.image-maps.com/`.

Getting ready

We are going to work with statistics of the nationality of our students in the school. We enter the names of the continents. If you happen to live in a cosmopolitan city, it would be very interesting! We add hyperlinks to websites displaying information about the continents.

How to do it...

In this recipe, we work with OpenOffice; another way to do it is to use similar software. So, we run OpenOffice Draw and perform the following steps to carry out the activity:

1. Click on **File | Save As....**Write a name for the file. Click on **Save**.
2. Click on **Insert | Chart**.
3. Right-click on the chart and choose **Chart Data Table...**, as shown in the following screenshot:

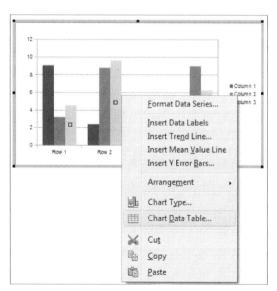

4. Complete the table with the information you want to display on the chart using the nationality of the students in the classroom or school.

5. Right-click again on the chart and choose **Chart Type**.

6. Choose **Pie | Exploded Donut Chart**.

7. Tick **3D Look**, as shown in the following screenshot:

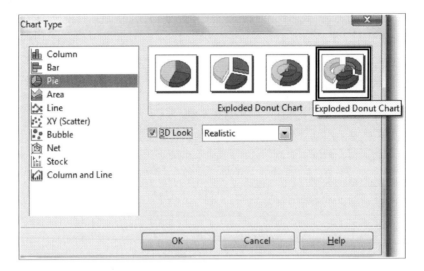

8. Click on **OK**.

9. Navigate to **Insert | Picture | From file**. Click on the image you want to insert. Click on **Open**.

10. Insert one image related to each continent for each piece of the chart.

11. Repeat steps 9 and 10 for each bar of the chart.

12. Click on the **Hyperlink** icon. Complete the block with hyperlinks related to each continent, as shown in the following screenshot:

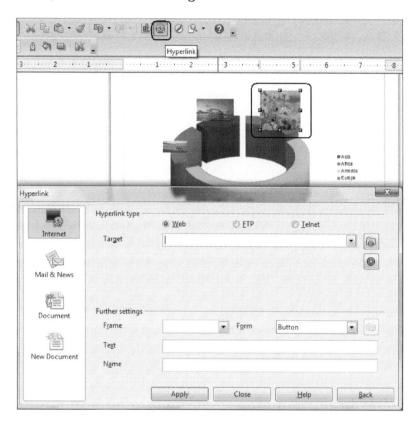

13. Repeat step 12 for the rest of the images.
14. Save the file.

How it works...

We have just designed a chart with hyperlinks using OpenOffice. We can insert it in our Moodle course as a resource. So, we can design an activity in several parts. You can make a survey to know the nationality of students if you happen not to have this information (as we have done in previous recipes). Then, you can create the chart using Draw in OpenOffice (that is your homework!) and add the file as a resource in the Moodle course. Finally, you can create an online text activity within assignments asking students which continent they find appealing to visit and why, based on the information displayed on the chart.

Designing a map chart

In this activity, we design a map chart. This chart is very appealing to our students due to the fact that it is not an ordinary one. We need to design it in Google Docs; we have already used this website in a previous recipe, so we have an account.

Getting ready

We can use the information in the previous recipe in this chart because we've worked with recording the nationality of our students; but, in this case, we need to concentrate on countries not continents. We need the name of the countries in order to design this map chart. So, let's get ready in order to create it!

How to do it...

We enter Google Docs and we sign into our account. Then, we need to perform the following steps in order to design a map chart:

1. Click on **Create | Spreadsheet**.
2. Design the chart using the information from the previous recipe. Another option is to design a chart using names of countries.
3. Select the data to draw the chart. Click on **Insert | Chart**.
4. The chart editor appears in a pop-up window.
5. Navigate to **Charts | Map | Insert**, as shown in the following screenshot:

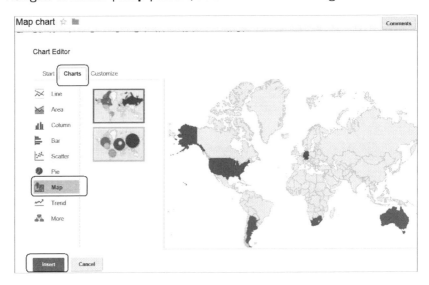

6. The map chart is ready!

How it works...

It is time to embed the charts in our Moodle course. One way to do it is by following the steps in the previous recipe to share the file; another option is to use Google+ to share the chart that we have designed. Then, we share the link in **Google+** in our Moodle course. So, perform the following steps:

1. Click on **Share**.
2. Click on the **Google+** icon, as shown in the following screenshot:

3. A pop-up window appears.

4. Add a comment, as shown in the following screenshot:

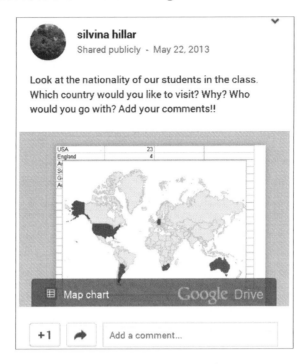

5. Click on **Share**.

6. Enter your Google+ account and see the post.

If you have a Google Docs account, you can share the account with Google+ so that the settings are the same once signed in with Google. Copy the URL and add a resource in the Moodle course so that students can enter their account on Google+ and share their ideas. In this case, we have to bear in mind privacy concerns, especially with younger students.

Creating a gauge chart

This is a very appealing chart because it is not an ordinary one. It is a very simple activity that we can carry out with any of the information that we have been working with. In this case, we are going to work with types of memory. So, let's get ready!

Getting ready

First of all, we need to collect the data in order to draw the chart. We have already designed several activities in which we can do it, although there are many more ways to do it. After gathering the necessary data to draw the chart, we need to sign in to Google Docs where we can find this type of chart.

How to do it...

We need to enter the website `http://populationaction.org/` and follow some steps in order to get the HTML code and embed it in our Moodle course. The following are the steps to follow:

1. Enter Google Docs and click on **Create | Spreadsheet**.

2. Click on **Untitled spreadsheet** and write the name of the file, as shown in the following screenshot:

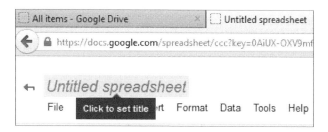

3. After gathering it, fill in the data to be used in order to draw the chart, as has been done in the previous recipes.

4. Select the data and click on **Insert | Chart**.

5. The chart editor appears in a pop-up window. Click on **More**, as shown in the following screenshot:

6. Click on **More | Gauge**, as shown in the following screenshot:

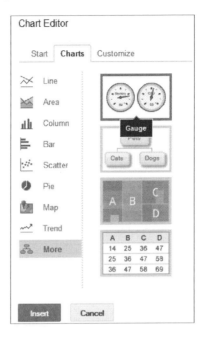

7. Click on **Insert**.

8. Click on **Share** on the top right-hand side.

9. Click on **Change** under **Who have access**.

10. Tick the **Anyone with the link** option. Click on **Save** and then **Done**.

11. Click on the down arrow in the chart and choose **Publish chart...**, as shown in the following screenshot:

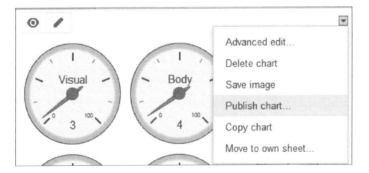

12. Click on the down arrow next to **Select a publish format** and choose **Image**.

13. Copy the HTML code.

14. Click on **Done**.

How it works...

It is time to embed the gauge charts in our Moodle course. We can design an assignment in which students have to find out how intelligences work. So, we choose the weekly outline section where we want to insert this activity and perform the following steps:

1. Click on **Add an activity or resource**.

2. Click on **Assignment | Add**.

3. Complete the **Assignment name** and **Description** blocks.

4. Click on the **Edit HTML source** icon.

5. Paste the HTML code which was copied.

6. Click on **Update**.

7. Tick **File submission** within **Submission types**.

8. Click on **Save and display**. The activity looks as shown in the following screenshot:

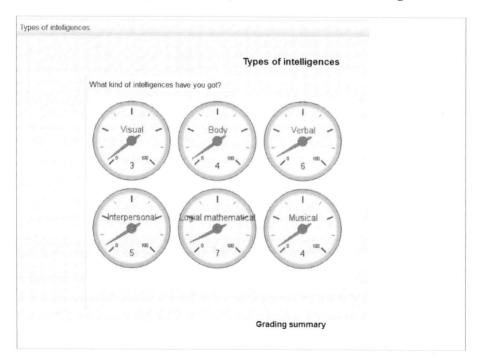

4
Integrating Interactive Documents

In this chapter, we will cover the following recipes:

- Developing collaborative writing exercises with Google Docs
- Using Flickr images in OpenOffice documents
- Including live PDF documents in Moodle
- Using Google Drive Voice Comments for online assignments
- Designing a collaborative wiki
- Sharing files with Office 365 Education
- Sharing a folder from Dropbox
- Working with files and folders within Moodle

Introduction

This chapter explains how to use different types of interactive documents in Moodle courses. The recipes use the most popular, free and commercial, web-based and desktop-based software to create interactive documents and provide students with the necessary information for their research activities.

Integrating interactive documents in our Moodle courses is a very important asset to take into account. Not only do students have the possibility to work with another tool to edit their work but they also learn how to store and share their work. Each of the following software to be considered in the foregoing recipes need to be eligible according to the type of activity to be carried out.

The baseline topic of this chapter will be *Fact or Fiction*. There are plenty of activities that can be carried out using this baseline topic. According to the subject that you are teaching, you can change the activities in such a way that you can adapt to the content of the recipe to design a multimedia activity in your Moodle courses.

Depending on the subject that you are teaching, or the type of activity that you want to design, you can combine these recipes with integrating interactive documents using any of the recipes in *Chapter 3, Working with Different Types of Interactive Charts*. As most of the recipes in this chapter use the same software, you can apply the tips and tricks you learned in the previous chapter.

Recipes are not only based on the different tools that the software has but also on several ways so that the students can take advantage of them. In other words, collaborative writing is also possible using those tools. These specific characteristics are to be pointed out in each of the recipes.

Moodle per se allows us to carry out activities in collaborative writing, but we are focusing on multimedia assets. Besides, students will be learning that there are plenty of options and many tools that can also be applied for integrating interactive documents.

Files should ideally have images in order to look more attractive. These images can be added from Flickr, which is an amazing website where we can look for many of them.

Another important element to take into account when designing files is the voice; we can add voice to our files! This is great because if we are teaching a foreign language or students with difficulties, it is an element that enhances the file. There are plenty of elements that we can take into account when designing files or writing activities for our students. Let's explore them.

Developing collaborative writing exercises with Google Docs

In this recipe, we deal with Google Docs because we want the students to deal with collaborative writing. There are plenty of options that can be carried out according to the type of activity that we want to design, that is to say, the way we can upload it into our Moodle course.

Getting ready

First of all, go to `https://drive.google.com/`. If you have already used this online software, you must have an account; otherwise, you have to sign up so as to create a document.

How to do it...

The topic to be covered in this recipe is Yeti because Fact or Fiction is the baseline topic that we will work with in this chapter. We can create the activity—the first part of the activity—in this document. What we want through this tool is for students to use Google Docs in a collaborative way. The following are the steps that you have to follow:

1. Enter your account in Google Docs.

2. Click on **Create | Document**.

3. Create a file that is to start a debate among students whether Yeti is a fact or fiction. You could create a link to a website that gives information about the creature, as shown in the following screenshot:

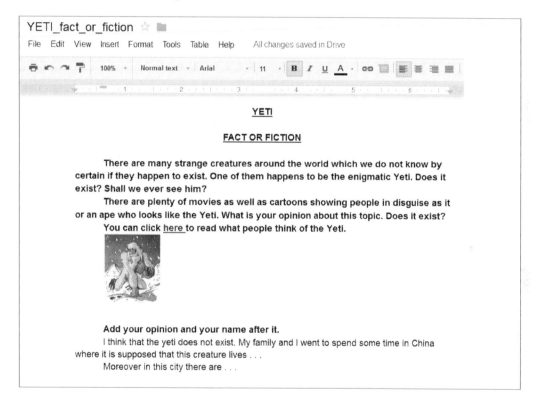

4. Write a name for the file and it will be saved automatically.

5. Click on **Share** on the top right-hand margin. Choose **Anyone with the link**.

6. Click on the down arrow next to **Access: Anyone (no sign-in required)** and select **Can edit**, as shown in the following screenshot:

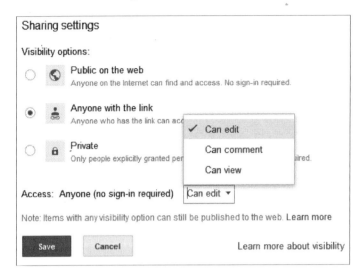

7. Click on **Save**.
8. Copy the URL to share the file.
9. Click on **Done**.

How it works...

We have just created the file that students can modify in a collaborative way. It is time to link it to our Moodle course. Choose the weekly outline section where you want to insert this resource and follow these steps:

1. Click on **Add an activity or resource**.
2. Click on **URL | Add**.
3. Complete the **Name** and the **Description** blocks.
4. Paste the URL that you copied from Google Docs in the **External URL** block within **Content**.
5. Click on the down arrow next to **Options**.
6. Click on **Display | Embed**.

7. Click on **Save and display**. The activity looks as shown in the following screenshot:

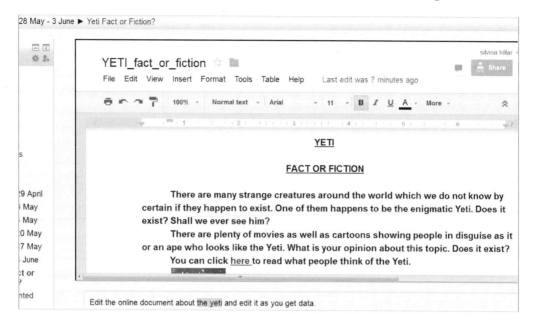

Using Flickr images in OpenOffice documents

In the previous chapter, we have already worked with OpenOffice, but in this chapter we are working with a text document. We are going to create a file and add images from Flickr. We will work with external files because OpenOffice does not have a clipart library. Thus, this tool is the right option.

Getting ready

We can both search for a photo in Flickr or upload a picture from our personal collection. However, I doubt that we have a photo of these creatures. Therefore, we need to visit http://www.flickr.com/ and create a free account, if you do not happen to have one already, and upload photos to our document in OpenOffice.

How to do it...

When we enter our Flickr account, we can search for photos that people have uploaded. Therefore, these are the steps we need to follow in order to find photos to insert in our OpenOffice file:

1. In the **search** block to the right, type `yeti` because we need photos of the said creature.

2. Click on the search block to the left and choose **Search Everyone's Uploads**, as shown in the following screenshot:

3. Click on the image that you want to insert in the file.

4. Right-click on the image and choose **Save Picture As**.

 Bear in mind that you need to select a free license image.

5. Another option is to right-click on the image, click on **Copy**, and then paste the image in the file in OpenOffice.

6. Repeat step 4 or 5 for each image you want to use.

How it works...

We have just selected the images that we need to upload to our document. We can upload them in two ways as explained previously in steps 4 and 5, though it would be better to save the image if we need it another time. So these are the steps that we have to follow:

1. Open the previous document in OpenOffice.

2. Navigate to **Insert | Picture | From file...**. Select the image that we want to use, and click on **Open**.

3. Enlarge or minimize the image so that it fits the desired size.

4. When the image appears in the file, you can use the picture toolbar to enhance it, as shown in the following screenshot:

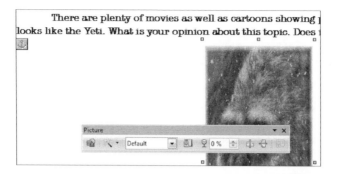

5. Another option is to right-click on the place where we want to paste the image and click on **Paste** if you have just copied the image from Flickr.

6. Repeat either step 2 or 5 as many times as you want to insert images, whether you copied or saved the image.

7. Click on **File | Save As...**. Write a name for the file, and click on **Save**. The file looks as shown in the following screenshot:

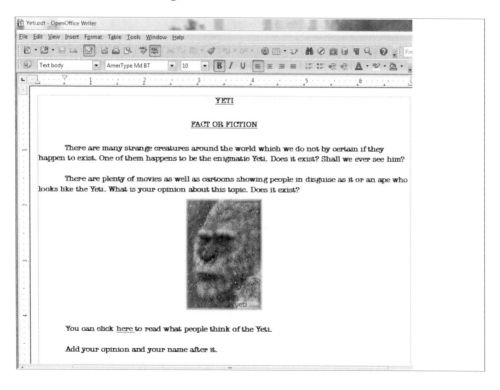

There's More

We will now see how the file we just created is uploaded to our Moodle course:

Uploading the file to our Moodle course

We have to upload the file that we have created in our Moodle course. We can add a resource, which is the simplest way to do it. We need to enter our Moodle course and choose the weekly outline section where we want to add the resource. So, there are a few more steps to follow in order to finish; let's follow them:

1. Click on **Add an activity or resource**.

2. Click on **File | Add**.

3. Complete the **Name** and **Description** blocks.

4. Click on **Add** within the content block, as shown in the following screenshot:

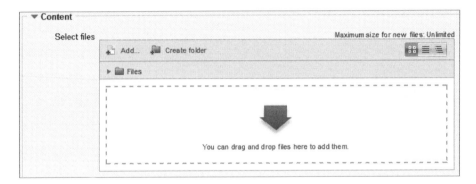

5. Navigate to **Upload a file | Browse**. Click on the file, then click on **Open**, and finally on **Upload**.

6. Click on **Save and display**; the resource looks as shown in the following screenshot:

Including live PDF documents in Moodle

This recipe is very interesting and appealing for our students. We can develop any type of activity using this resource because we are inserting a live PDF within our Moodle course. In older versions of Moodle, we had to work out some code; however, in Moodle 2.5, we have the possibility to embed the file in a much easier way.

We can include a live PDF by just uploading a file. So, it means that the toolbar which allows us to save or print the PDF appears when hovering the mouse over the file.

Getting ready

We can work with any text editor or word processor that allows us to convert the file into PDF; another option is to work with an already designed PDF. So, we work with OpenOffice in order to convert a file that we have just designed into PDF. We use the same file to avoid creating a new one.

The software that we need for this recipe is Adobe Reader, which can be downloaded from `http://get.adobe.com/reader/`.

How to do it...

First of all, we need to convert a file into PDF. Therefore, we choose the file used in the previous recipe; the steps are similar in any text software so follow them in order to convert it:

1. Enter **OpenOffice** and click on **Text Document**.
2. Navigate to **File | Open** and browse for the file that we want to convert into PDF.

3. Navigate to **File** | **Export as PDF** | **Export**, as shown in the following screenshot:

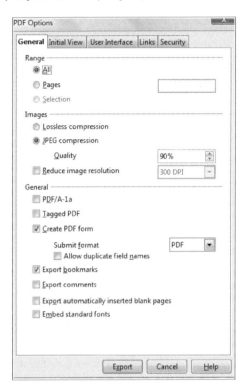

4. Write a name for the file and click on **Save**.

5. You can now open the file using Adobe Reader.

How it works...

We have just converted a file into PDF. As we embed it, we need to upload the file as a resource. We can also embed live PDF in any activity working with the HTML code, but as Moodle 2.5 offers the possibility to embed the file by just a few clicks, we add a resource. These are the steps that we have to follow:

1. Click on **Add an activity or resource**.

2. Click on **File** | **Add**.

3. Complete the **Name** and **Description** blocks.

4. Click on **Options**.

5. Click on the down arrow next to **Display**. Click on **Embed**, as shown in the following screenshot:

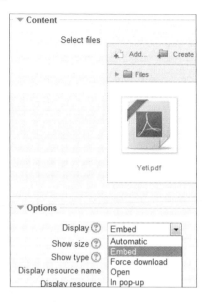

6. Click on **Save and display**; the file looks as shown in the following screenshot:

Embedding Adobe files working with HTML code

We have converted a file into PDF and uploaded it to the Moodle course as a file. There is another way to do it working with some code. We are going to create an activity; in this instance, we will create an **Online text** activity but you can choose any other. Choose the weekly outline section to add the activity and follow these steps:

1. Click on **Add an activity or resource**.

2. Click on **Assignments | Add**.

3. Complete the **Assignment name** and **Description** blocks.

4. In the **Description** block, highlight some words and click on the **Insert/edit link** icon.

5. Click on **Browse** within the **Link URL** block, as shown in the following screenshot:

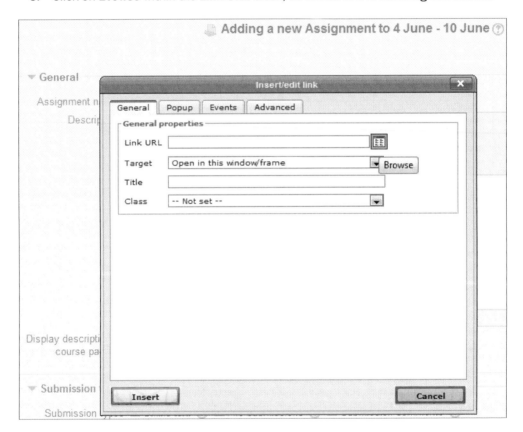

6. Click on **Upload a file | Browse**. Click on the file to upload and then on **Open**. Upload this file and then click on **Insert**.

7. We have just created a link to the PDF file.

8. Click on the **Edit HTML source** icon and write the following code to it:

```
<embed src="FullScreenEmbed.pdf" width="800" height="500">
```

9. Change some information of the code. That is to say, add the name of the file that we have just uploaded instead of `FullScreenEmbed.pdf`, as follows:

```
<embed
src="http://localhost/draftfile.php/13/user/draft/387786865
/Yeti_and_Bigfoot.pdf"width="800" height="500">
```

10. Click on **Update**.

11. Click on **Online text** within the **Submission types** block.

12. Click on **Save and display**. It looks as shown in the following screenshot:

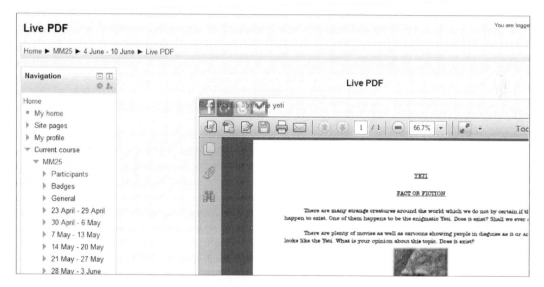

Using Google Drive Voice Comments for online assignments

In this recipe, we work with Google Docs, and we can add our voice to these documents. We can also share the file using Google+ and save it in Google Drive. As we add voice comments to the file, we create a special account for students to work with. It will be an account for a specific purpose that works with voice as well.

Getting ready

The voice comments in Google Docs is, at the moment of writing this book, only available for teachers and not for students. This is the reason why we create a special account for students to share not only the writing, but also their voice in an assignment. When talking and recording the comments, we can also highlight the words, phrases, or sentences that we want to spot out, with different colors. Let's see how to do it.

 Remember to create a special account and share its e-mail address and password with students. The idea is to share both the writing and the voice recording in the same file. Students will find it very appealing.

How to do it...

We work with the file that we have already designed in previous recipes. If we create another account, we can copy and save the file in the new account.

The first thing that we have to do is to enable our voice comments in the new account in order to use it. It is an advantage due to the fact that many students do not read comments, besides, correcting is much faster and we can provide feedback in a more effective way. These are the steps that we have to follow:

1. Open your default web browser and sign in to the Google account to share with students.

2. Navigate to **Drive | Create | Connect more apps**, as shown in the following screenshot:

3. Click on **Voice Comments**, as shown in the following screenshot:

4. Click on **Connect**.

5. Go back to the home page where all the files are listed.

6. Hover the mouse over the file to open and right-click on it. Then, click on **Open with** and select **Kaizena**, as shown in the following screenshot:

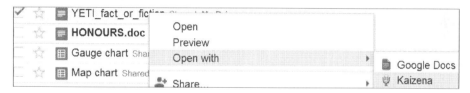

7. Click on **Allow access**.

8. Click on **Rec** to record your voice comments. Pause it when necessary.

9. If you need to highlight words, click on the desired color to highlight the text, as shown in the following screenshot:

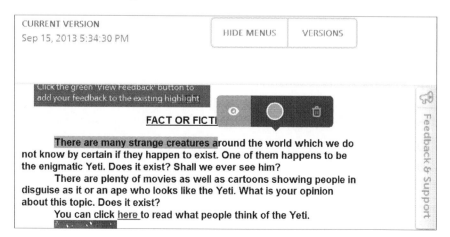

10. When you finish recording, click on the play button to check. You can also delete the recording by clicking on the bin icon.

11. You can share the comments if you have connections in your Google+ account, which is on the left-hand side of the margin.

12. Copy the URL of the file in order to upload it to our Moodle course, as shown in the following screenshot:

How it works...

There are plenty of advantages when working with sounds because students can listen to them and read at the same time. Apart from this, when teaching a foreign language, they can not only listen to the comments in this language but also work in the immersion of it, listening and reading in the language that the student learns. Let's upload the new resource in our Moodle course. Follow these steps to do so:

1. Click on **Add an activity or resource**.

2. Click on **URL | Add**.

3. Complete the **Name** and the **Description** blocks (remember to add the e-mail address and password of the special account created).

4. Paste the URL that you copied in step 12 (in the _How to do it..._ section) in the **External URL** block within **Content**.

5. Click on the down arrow next to **Options**.

6. Click on **Display | Embed**.

7. Click on **Save and display**.

8. After the students sign in, the activity looks as shown in the following screenshot:

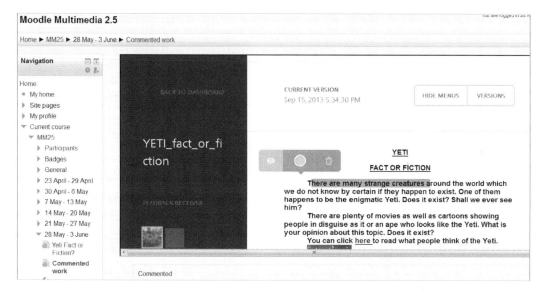

 Students can also receive voice comments if the information is shared through Google+, and the files can be shared. In this instance, privacy matters are to be an issue depending on the age of the students.

Designing a collaborative wiki

There is another interesting and different way of creating collaborative writing, that is, designing a wiki using the website http://www.wikispaces.com/. It enhances students' way of learning; as teachers, use several resources in order to avoid routine. Another option is to use wikis within our Moodle course.

Getting ready

In this website we can create either activities or projects. There is a possibility to work with HTML code as well, so when designing an activity, we can take these assets into account in order to embed them to the page that we create.

How to do it...

We need to create an account in the already mentioned website. We can create a classroom within it, and the account is free for educators. So, these are the steps that we have to follow:

1. Enter `http://www.wikispaces.com/` in the browser window.

2. Click on **I'm a Teacher**, as shown in the following screenshot:

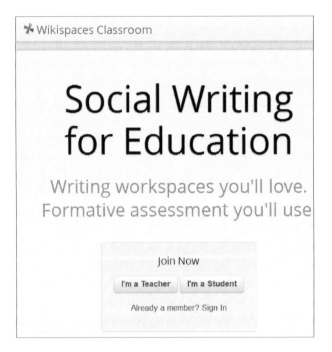

3. Complete all the necessary information in order to create the account.

4. Click on **New Wiki** on the top right-hand margin to start designing the wiki.

5. Click on the down arrow within the **Your Industry** block and choose **K-12 Education**, as shown in the following screenshot:

6. Click on **Continue**.
7. Write a name for the wiki next to the **wikispaces.com** block.
8. Complete the necessary fields and then click on **Create**.
9. On the right-hand margin, click on **Pages | Pages and Files**, as shown in the following screenshot:

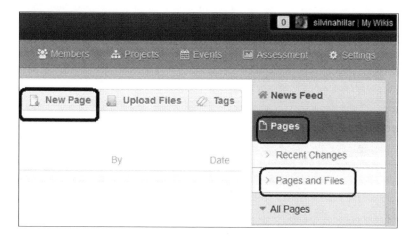

10. Click on **New Page**, as shown in the previous screenshot.
11. Complete the **Page Name** and **Add Tags** blocks.
12. Click on **Create**.

13. An editor appears in order to create the wiki. The editor is shown in the following screenshot:

14. The editor is similar to any editor that we have been working with; the only different item to take special attention of is **Widgets**. When we click on the said icon, the following widgets would appear that we can add to our wiki, as shown in the following screenshot:

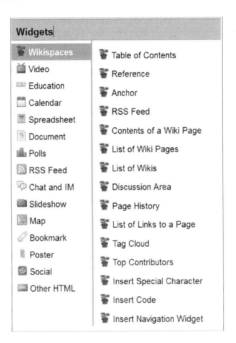

15. We can add any of these widgets to our **Wiki**. The instructions are shown when we click on any of these items. Many multimedia assets can easily be uploaded to the wiki.

16. After designing the wiki, click on **Preview** in case you need to edit something.

17. When the wiki is ready click on **Save**.

18. Navigate to **Settings | Permissions | Protected**, as shown in the following screenshot:

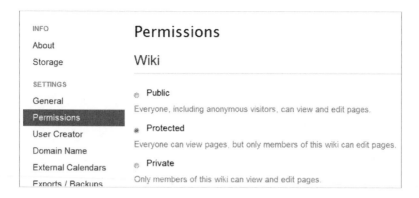

19. Click on **Update**.
20. Click on the name of the wiki **onlinedocuments** (in this case) on the left-hand margin and copy the URL.

 There are plenty of features that could take a whole chapter to be explored, but that is not the aim of the book; it is just to let you know how to design a wiki using a website. We can also create projects which is a new feature in order to create a classroom or an online course by just clicking on the project.

How it works...

We have just designed our wiki. It is time to embed it in our Moodle course. We can either design an activity or create a resource because the wiki that we have just created is part of an activity. Students should also write about their opinions after discussing them with their classmates. Therefore, enter the Moodle course and choose the weekly outline section to upload the resource. Follow these steps to do so:

1. Click on **Add an activity or resource**.
2. Click on **URL | Add**.
3. Complete the **Name** and **Description** blocks.
4. Paste the URL in the **External URL** block within **Content**.
5. Click on the drop-down menu next to **Options**.
6. Click on the drop-down menu next to **Display** and click on **Embed**.

7. Click on **Save and display**; the activity looks as shown in the following screenshot:

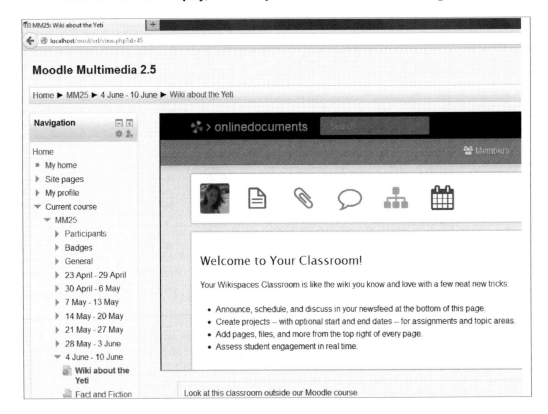

Sharing files with Office 365 Education

In previous recipes, we have dealt with Google Docs because we want students to write in a collaborative way. There is another option to work in the same way using Office 365 Education; the difference is that it is a commercial product with a discount for educational institutions. The advantages are that you can share the file just as you did in Google Docs.

Getting ready

First of all, visit the website `http://office.microsoft.com/en-us/academic/` in order to get a free trial of Office 365 Education. We need to click on **Try now** and follow the tutorial wizard in order to create the account. It is shown in the following screenshot:

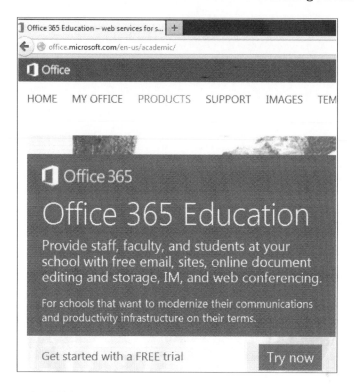

How to do it...

After creating the account and having access to the free trial, we can create an online document to share with students. We can create a document in which students work in a collaborative way. These are the steps to follow:

1. Enter your account in Office 365.
2. Click on **MY OFFICE** in the upper ribbon.

3. Click on **Word document** under **Create new**, as shown in the following screenshot:

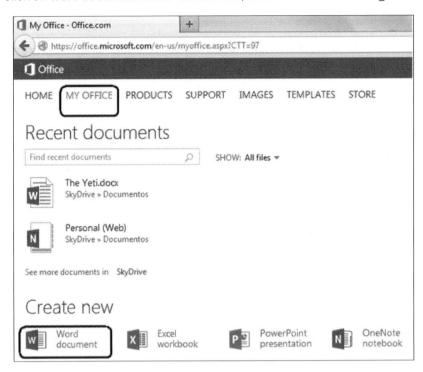

4. Type a name for the file and click on **Create**, as shown in the following screenshot:

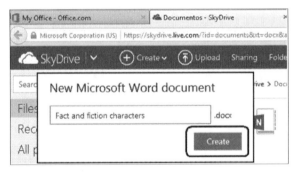

5. Design the file as if you were using MS Word.

6. Click on **SHARE** in the upper ribbon.

7. There is a pop-up window. Click on **Get a link**. The options are similar to the ones in Google Docs.

8. Click on **Make public**.

9. Copy the link (you can shorten the link).

10. Click on **Close**, as shown in the following screenshot:

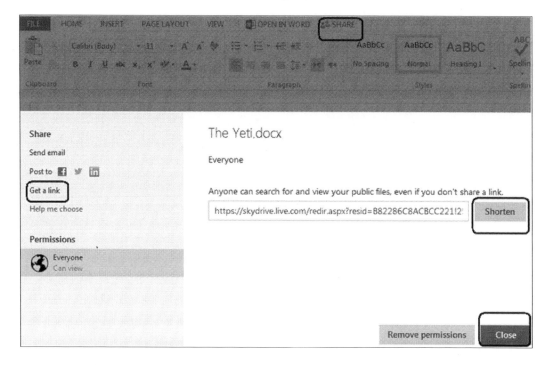

How it works...

We have just created the file in Office 365 that students can modify in a collaborative way. They can also have the option to open it in MS Word. The remaining task of the recipe is to link it to our Moodle course. Choose the weekly outline section where you want to insert this resource and follow these steps:

1. Click on **Add an activity or resource**.

2. Click on **Assignment | Add**.

3. Complete the **Assignment name** block.

4. Complete the **Description** block and make a link to the file that was created in Office 365.

5. Click on the **Insert/edit link** icon.

6. Paste the URL in the **Link URL** block.

7. Click on **Insert**.

8. Within **Submission types** click on **Online text**.

9. Click on **Save and display**; the activity looks as shown in the following screenshot:

Sharing a folder from Dropbox

This is a very interesting recipe because we share files from Dropbox. It is a place where we can store our files, videos, and images in order to make a backup as well. We can upload and share the files that we have there. Another feature is that we can also share a complete folder, not only the files.

Getting ready

First of all, visit the website `https://www.dropbox.com/` in order to create an account in Dropbox. The only person who needs the account is the teacher, but you can also recommend students to have an account so that you can share folders and files easily. We can have Dropbox installed on mobile devices, which is important nowadays.

How to do it...

After creating an account in Dropbox, we have to create a folder and upload files in order to share it in our Moodle course. The advantage of uploading files on an external website rather than in Moodle is that it does not occupy storage from the site. This is one of the main reasons to use different software in this chapter, that is, to broaden the opportunities. To upload a folder from Dropbox, these are the steps that you have to follow:

1. Visit your Dropbox account and sign in.

2. Click on the **New folder** icon, as shown in the following screenshot:

3. Write a name for the new folder.

4. Click on the folder to open it.

5. Navigate to **Upload** | **basic uploader** | **Choose files**. Click on the file to upload and then click on **Open**.

6. Repeat step 5 as many times as the number of files we need to upload.

7. When you finish uploading files, right-click on the folder and click on **Share link**, as shown in the following screenshot:

8. Click on **Get link**.

9. Copy the URL to paste in our Moodle course.

10. You can also share the folder via e-mail, Facebook, or Twitter.

How it works...

Once we have copied the link of the folder from the Dropbox account, we can paste it in our Moodle course in order to share it. We have already pasted many links to files in previous recipes, so the process is the same. We can add a variety of activities and make a link to the folder, or add a resource and use the URL option in order to embed it in our Moodle course. When students click on the link, they can see the files within the folder that we have just created. If they have an account in Dropbox and a mobile device, they can download the files and read them there.

Working with files and folders within Moodle

In the last recipe of the chapter, we work on uploading files and folders within our Moodle course. We can do it very easily because uploading files or folders is just a few clicks away. So, let's get ready and think about which files we can upload in the Moodle course to use this resource.

Getting ready

We can upload files from our computer or from any website where we can store them. If we choose to do it from a website, we need to enable the repository to do it. We will work with repositories in *Chapter 9, Designing and Integrating Repositories and E-portfolios*, but the first option is the one that we are dealing with in this chapter.

How to do it...

In this recipe we just upload some files as resources to our Moodle course, so it is very simple. We have been working in many ways to perform the same process and keep the files away but linked to our Moodle course; now it is time to pay attention to Moodle itself. Choose the weekly outline section where we want to insert the resource and follow these steps to upload files into our Moodle course:

1. Click on **Add an activity or resource**.
2. Click on **File | Add**.
3. Complete the **Name** and **Description** blocks.
4. Click on **Add**, as shown in the following screenshot:

5. Click on **Upload a file** | **Browse**. Look for the file to upload (in this case, a presentation about a factual or a fictional creature). Click on the file to upload by navigating to **Open** | **Upload this file**.

6. Click on **Save** and return to the course. The resource has been uploaded to the course.

[Students must have installed the software in which the file has been created.]

How it works...

We have uploaded a file within our Moodle course. We can also upload a zipped folder which contains numerous files, for example, many essays written by different students. Another option is to create a folder in the Moodle course in order to organize the files; it all depends on the type of resource we want to upload. Choose the weekly outline section where we want to insert the resource and follow these steps:

1. Click on **Add an activity or resource**.

2. Click on **Folder** | **Add**, as shown in the following screenshot:

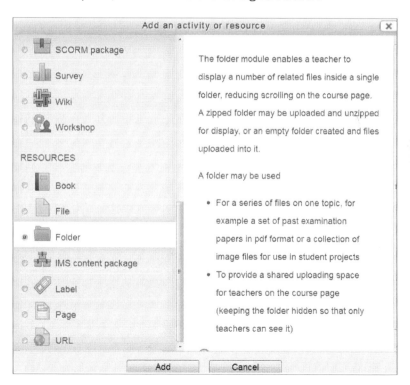

3. Complete the **Name** and the **Description** blocks.

4. Navigate to **Add | Upload a file | Browse**. Look for the zipped file to upload (in this case, a zipped folder of past essays and images about a factual or a fictional creature). Click on the file to upload and navigate to **Open | Upload this file**.

5. Click on **Save and return to course**. The resource has been uploaded to the Moodle course.

5
Working with Audio, Sound, Music, and Podcasts

In this chapter, we will cover the following recipes:

- ▸ Recording audio from a microphone
- ▸ Creating and embedding a podcast using SoundCloud
- ▸ Using VoiceThread to record presentations
- ▸ Embedding a presentation in VoiceThread in Moodle
- ▸ Using LibriVox to embed an audiobook
- ▸ Allowing a student to record audio

Introduction

This chapter explains how to work with different types of audio files to include sounds, music, and podcasts to Moodle courses. These recipes will teach you how to use different tools to record, edit, and convert different audio file formats, covering common scenarios for multimedia Moodle activities.

The sense of hearing plays an important role in learning a language due to the fact that there are plenty of students whose ability to learn depends on their musical intelligence. Besides, inserting this type of multimedia into our activities makes them more interesting to our students.

We can combine several pieces of recording with not only our own voice, but also somebody else's or with different sounds in the background. This way, podcasts won't be dull for students like when they have to listen only to the teacher speaking. The mixture of sounds, audio, and music is interesting because students can listen to small pieces of recordings or music, as well as us explaining what they are hearing.

Podcasting is an excellent way to share different elements with students. We can combine parts of recordings to make it possible for our students to listen to them as if they were radio shows created by their own teacher, depending on how creative we can be. Once we are confident with podcasts, we can enhance them easily.

Students can record their podcasts too. Some of the skills that students develop by creating podcasts include writing scripts and listening and speaking skills. They learn how to speak better because they have to pay attention to what they listen to. It is advised that students listen to our podcasts first and then make their own.

The baseline topic of this chapter is music and sounds around the world. Therefore, in our recipes, we will design several types of activities in which we need to use audio. We can combine several types of ingredients to make our recipes quite spicy!

The software that we use to create the podcast is **Audacity**. It is free and open source and works with several operating systems (OSes), such as Windows and Macintosh, among others. Therefore, we can use it no matter which OS we run in our computers. It is a very nice tool to explore because we can enhance our skills in the art of podcasting if we learn to use it.

An interesting type of audio file is MIDI. Unfortunately, Moodle 2.5 does not work with MIDI files at the time this book is being written; one option is to convert MIDI files to MP3 files and upload them to our Moodle course. This is a step that can be taken in case we are fond of these types of files.

Later on in the chapter, we learn how to allow students to record audio after listening to us speaking; now, it's time for us to listen to them. We can create this type of activity to make our virtual classroom more vivid. Thus, students practise other skills in previous chapters which they can use when they have to record themselves.

We also take a look at an interesting feature of Moodle, which is to create podcasts in the cloud. After creating the podcast, we can edit, download, or embed it. We can also share it using social networks. So, there are plenty of resources to work with sounds; we just have to think of an interesting activity or resource to design.

Recording audio from a microphone

In this recipe, we will learn how to record our voice using a microphone, as well as free and open source software which works with several OSes. Therefore, this software, can not only record live audio but also convert tapes and records into digital recordings, among other features it offers for our Moodle courses. We should also be aware of the fact that some material might be copyright protected.

Getting ready

We will record audio using a microphone and the Audacity software. It can be downloaded from `http://audacity.sourceforge.net/download/`. We have to bear in mind that this software works with different OSes; therefore, download only for the OS that is installed in your computer.

How to do it...

First, we download and install Audacity 2.0.2 on our computer. Then, we record ourselves to design a part of the activity to be added into our Moodle course; we can narrate an activity or something that is more interesting to listen to than read. For example, as the baseline topic of this chapter is music and sounds around the world, we can focus on the different accents in spoken English. Therefore, perform the following steps to design the activity:

1. Start Audacity.

2. Click on the **Record** button within the **Audio Control and Editing Toolbars** section, as shown in the following screenshot:

3. When you finish recording, click on the **Stop** button.

4. The digital representation of the voice (in wave form) is shown in the audio track portion within the Project view, as shown in the following screenshot:

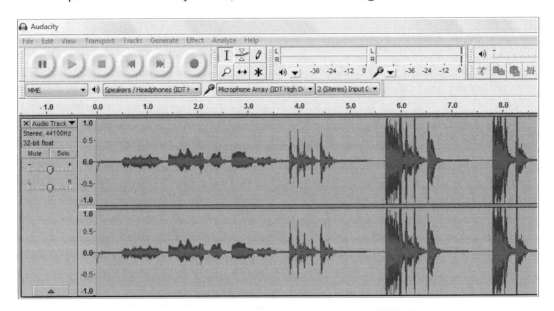

5. Click on **File | Save Project As...**, as shown in the following screenshot:

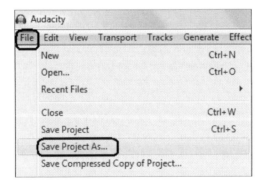

6. There appears a pop-up window indicating that the project is saved as `.aup` and you'll need to export the file to use it in different formats. Click on **OK**.

7. Write a name for the file and click on **Save**.

8. Click on **File | Export...**, and save the file as WAV type (or MP3); now, you can embed the file in our Moodle course. It is shown in the following screenshot:

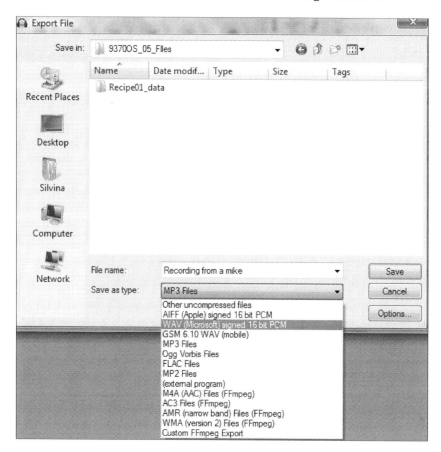

9. Click on **Save | OK**.

How it works...

We have just recorded a narration of an activity for our Moodle course, to which students have to listen in order to learn about English accents around the world. Therefore, we need to upload it to our Moodle course. To do this, choose the weekly outline section where you want to insert it and perform the following steps:

1. Click on **Add an activity or resource**.

2. Select **Assignment** and then click on **Add**.

3. Complete the **Assignment name** and the **Description** blocks.

4. Click on the **Show editing tools** tab just above the top-left corner of the **Description** block. Then, navigate to the **Insert Moodle media** icon (in the bottom row, fifth from the right) | **Find or upload a sound, video or applet ...** | **Upload a file** | **Browse**, look for the file that you want to upload, and select it. Remember to upload the file with the WAV extension, as shown in the following screenshot:

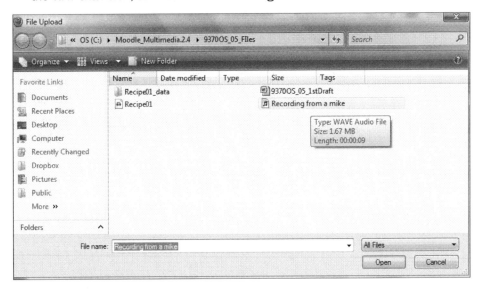

5. Click on **Open** | **Upload this file** | **Insert**.

6. Check the **Online text** checkbox within **Submission types**.

7. Click on **Save and display**; the activity looks as shown in the following screenshot:

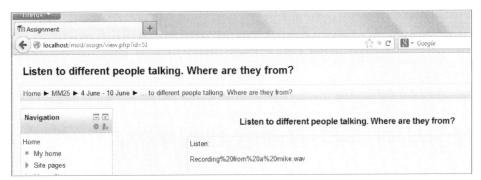

8. When students click on the name of the file, they will see a media player toolbar, as shown in the following screenshot:

9. When students click on the Play icon, they will listen to the recording.

10. You can create another activity to allow students to work with this resource.

Creating and embedding a podcast using SoundCloud

In the previous recipe, we learned how to record a sound using Audacity; in this recipe, we learn how to record and embed a podcast using `https://soundcloud.com/`. It is very simple and we do not have to install anything at all; we record it on the Web. After recording, we can embed the file or make a link to the recording in order to embed it in our Moodle course.

Getting ready

In order to get ready to work with SoundCloud, we need to create an account. We can sign up in the traditional way by following the wizard or connect with our Facebook or Google+ account.

As we have worked with Google+ in previous chapters, we can sign in with that account. Enter `https://soundcloud.com/`, click on **Sign up for SoundCloud**, and there will appear a pop-up window; click on **Sign in with Google**, as shown in the following screenshot:

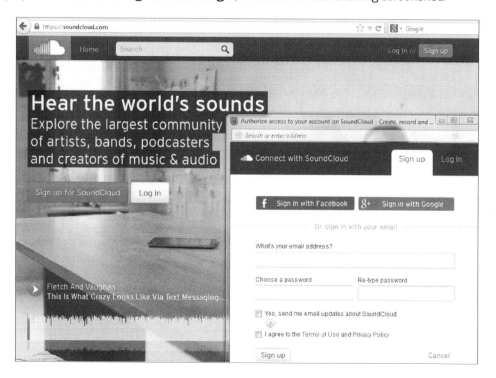

How to do it...

We have already logged in to SoundCloud, so now it's time to start designing our podcast. We can record or upload sounds in the order in which we create them. (We have to make sure that we have the Adobe Flash plugin installed in our browser.) In this case, we are going to record; so, to design the podcast, perform the following steps:

1. Click on **Upload** at the top-right margin, as shown in the following screenshot:

2. Click on the **Start new recording** button; a new window will open.

3. Click on the **REC** button.

4. Click on **Allow**, as shown in the following screenshot:

5. You might have to click on the **REC** button again if the recording doesn't start and the browser might ask your permission to access your microphone device; let the browser access it. When you finish recording, click on **Upload your recording**, as shown in the following screenshot:

6. Complete the **Title** block.

7. There are other blocks present; filling information in them is optional.

8. Scroll down. Within **Settings**, make the podcast **Public** so that it can be embedded, as shown in the following screenshot:

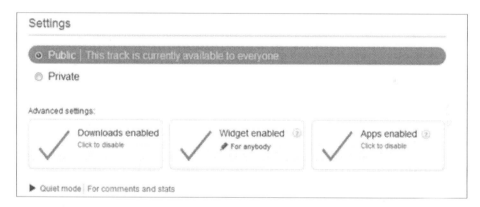

9. Click on **Save**.

10. Click on **Share** and copy the code present in the **Widget Code** textbox to paste it in the Moodle course, as shown in the following screenshot:

How it works...

We have just recorded a podcast on the web. Another option is to upload a podcast that we have in our computer to SoundCloud. It is time to embed the podcast in our Moodle course. Choose the weekly outline section where we want to upload the activity and perform the following steps:

1. Click on **Add an activity or resource**.

2. Select **Label** and then click on **Add**.

3. Complete the **Label text** block.

4. Click on the **Show editing tools** tab just above the top-left corner of the **Label text** block, then, click on the last icon and the **Edit HTML source** icon, and then paste the code we copied earlier in the **HTML source editor** window; then, click on **Update**.

5. Click on **Save and return to course**; the resource appears, as shown in the following screenshot:

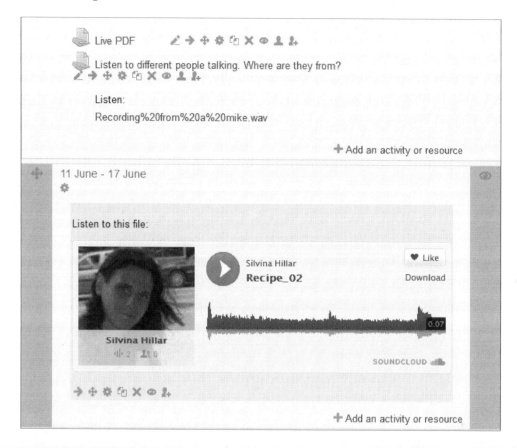

Using VoiceThread to record presentations

VoiceThread has plenty of uses; one of them is relevant to this chapter. It is a tool for collaborative commenting using audio online. Another usage of VoiceThread is video. It can be easily integrated in Moodle because we can use HTML code to do it. It is also interesting to add visual information on several topics.

Getting ready

In order to use VoiceThread, we need to create an account with the website https://voicethread.com/. We need to click on **Register** at the top-right margin and enter the necessary information to create the account. After signing in, we can enjoy working with VoiceThread!

How to do it...

There are many ways that we can use VoiceThread, apart from voice recording. It is really an amazing tool to explore and could be added to any recipe of the book covering the different multimedia features, but we are going to focus on the audio. On the upper ribbon, there is an option that reads **Ideas for using VoiceThread**, which is very interesting.

Let's focus on audio and creating a resource for students to add audio to. The following are the steps that we have to follow:

1. After signing in, click on **Create**.

2. Click on **Upload**. Within **Upload** there appear many items to choose from.

3. Click on **My Computer**, as shown in the following screenshot:

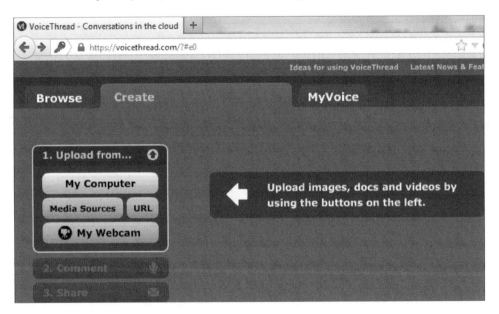

4. Upload images or the desired resource. Select the file to upload and click on **Open**.

5. Repeat steps 3 and 4 as many times as the number of files you need to upload.

6. Click on **Comment**, as shown in the following screenshot:

7. Click on **record**. It appears under the file just uploaded, as shown in the following screenshot:

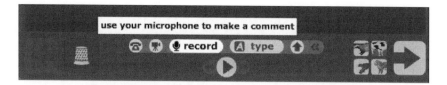

8. Click on **Allow**. Your browser might ask for your permission to allow access to your microphone; grant it access.
9. Start recording the presentation.
10. Click on the sideways arrow to insert the images or files uploaded.
11. Click on **Stop recording** when the recording is complete.
12. Click on **record more**, if needed.
13. When the recording is complete, click on **save**, as shown in the following screenshot:

How it works...

We have just recorded our voice in the presentation. There are some more steps that we have to follow in order to complete the process. We need to create a group of our VoiceThread instances in order to be found. We have to ask students to add their voices to our presentation. In this presentation, we can find 3D images of animals that are typical of different countries and students have to spot the way people speak English in them. It can also be a non-English speaking country where English is the second most-spoken language or not spoken there at all. Let's see what students have to say!

The following are the steps that you have to follow in order to finish the presentation:

1. Click on **(Add a title and description)**.
2. A pop-up window appears; complete the necessary blocks.
3. Click on **Save**.
4. Click on **Publishing Options** within the options in the menu at the bottom of the page.

5. Check the **Allow anyone to View** and **Allow anyone to Comment** blocks, as shown in the following screenshot:

6. Click on **save**.

See also

▶ The *Embedding a presentation in VoiceThread using Moodle* recipe

Embedding a presentation in VoiceThread using Moodle

It is time to embed a resource in our Moodle course. So, we have to think of an activity from the VoiceThread presentation that we have designed. Another option is to ask students to design their presentation in VoiceThread. So, let's get ready!

Getting ready

It is advisable to ask students to register in VoiceThread, so that they can add their voice comments to the presentation that we have designed. Another possibility is that students design a presentation and we add our voice comments. In both cases, students and teachers must have an account to add comments.

How to do it...

We need to work on the VoiceThread that we have designed in the previous recipe to get a link or HTML code in order to embed it in our Moodle course. We enter the VoiceThread website and sign in.

1. Click on the **MyVoice** tab and select the presentation we have already made.

2. Click on **Menu** at the top left-hand margin, as shown in the following screenshot:

3. Click on **Share**. There appear many options to share the VoiceThread presentation.

4. Click on **Embed**. The HTML code appears. (You can also share the presentation using Facebook or Twitter.)

5. Click on **Copy this**, which is next to the **Embed code** textbox. There appears a sign stating **Copied to clipboard**, as shown in the following screenshot:

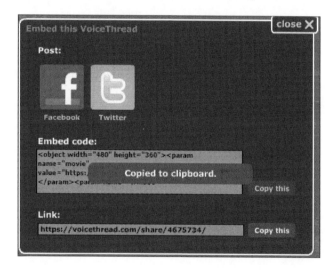

6. Click on **close**.

How it works...

We already copied the embed code, so now we have to paste it in our Moodle course. We can design a label which is great to display or embed a sound file or video in our course. We can add a short note telling students to register in VoiceThread so that they can add voice comments. The following are the steps to follow:

1. Click on **Add an activity or resource**.

2. Select **Label** and then click on **Add**.

3. Complete the **Label text** block.

4. Click on the **Show editing tools** tab just above the top-left corner of the **Label text** block, and then click on the last icon, the **Edit HTML source** icon. Paste the embed code we copied earlier in the **HTML source editor** window and then, click on **Update**.

5. Click on **Save and return to course**; the resource appears, as shown in the following screenshot:

Using LibriVox to embed an audiobook

LibriVox provides free audiobooks from a public domain; so, this means that we can use it to embed them in our Moodle course. There are two options: either listen to audiobooks or read and record chapters. So, this is a great resource for an English or Literature teacher, or any other teacher willing to use this amazing resource.

Getting ready

Before embedding an audiobook in our Moodle course, we have to think about which book to use; so, let's visit the website `http://librivox.org/` and look for the book that we have in mind and see if we can find it.

How to do it...

LibriVox offers a variety of languages in which books can be listened to, so it is also very important for a foreign language teacher to use this resource. Before embedding the audiobook in our Moodle course, we need to get the MP3 file. So, the following are the steps that we need to follow:

1. Enter the `http://librivox.org/` website.
2. Click on **CATALOG**.
3. Click on **Title**.
4. Fill in the search block, as shown in the following screenshot:

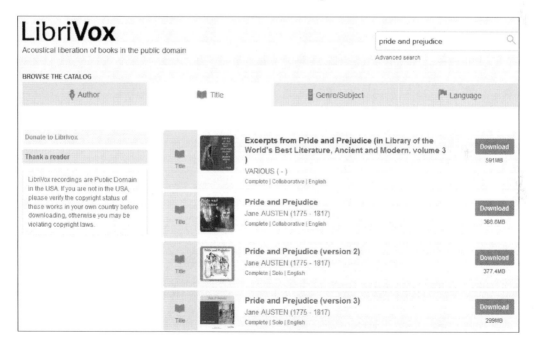

5. Click on the search icon.

6. In this case, there appears several options click on the desired one—in this case **Pride and Prejudice: A Play**—as shown in the following screenshot:

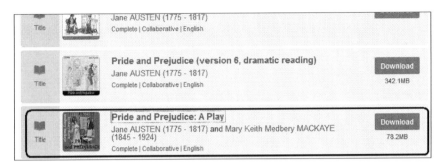

7. Click on **Internet Archive Page** under **Links** on the left-hand margin, as shown in the following screenshot:

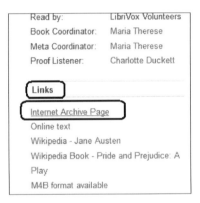

8. Click on the icon that appears at the top-right margin of the player, as shown in the following screenshot:

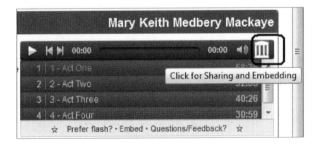

9. Copy the **Embed code** that appears, as shown in the following screenshot:

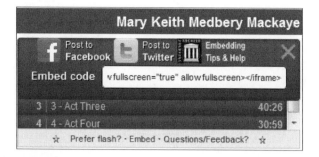

How it works...

Now that we've copied the embed code, we can embed this file in our Moodle course. We can create a resource and, afterwards, an activity in which students listen to the book or some chapters from the book. Next, they may do another activity related to the book or the country where the story takes place. So, choose the weekly outline section where we want to add this activity and perform the following steps to embed the files from LibriVox:

1. Click on **Add an activity or resource**.
2. Select **Label** and then click on **Add**.
3. Complete the **Label text** block.
4. Click on the **Show editing tools** tab just above the top-left corner of the **Label text** block, click on the last icon, the **Edit HTML source** icon, and paste the embed code that we copied before in the **HTML source editor** window; then click on **Update**.
5. Click on **Save and return to course**; the activity looks as shown in the following screenshot:

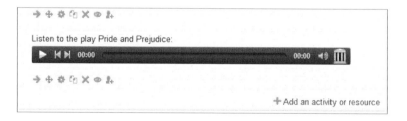

Allowing students to record audio

This is a very simple recipe that can be carried out using Moodle assignments, that is, through uploading files. It means that students are going to record their own voices and we can listen to their recording through the file that they upload. We can set guidelines so that students know how to create their recording.

Getting ready

It is time for our students to take a deep breath and talk. Now, we have to be clear in the way we ask them to say what we want to hear. Taking into account that our baseline topic in this chapter is music and sounds around the world, we can ask students to talk in their own English accent as the accent varies across different parts of the world.

How to do it...

Students can record themselves using either devices, such as their mobile phones or the Audacity software for creating audio files. We should ask them to upload their recordings as .mp3 or .wav files, as well as state other important guidelines, such as time and information. Perform the following steps to design the activity:

1. Click on **Add an activity or resource**.
2. Select **Assignment** and then click on **Add**.
3. Complete the **Assignment name** and **Description** blocks. Set the guidelines clearly so that students know what they have to record.
4. Check the **File submissions** checkbox within **Submission types**.

5. Click on **Save and display**. The activity appears, as shown in the following screenshot:

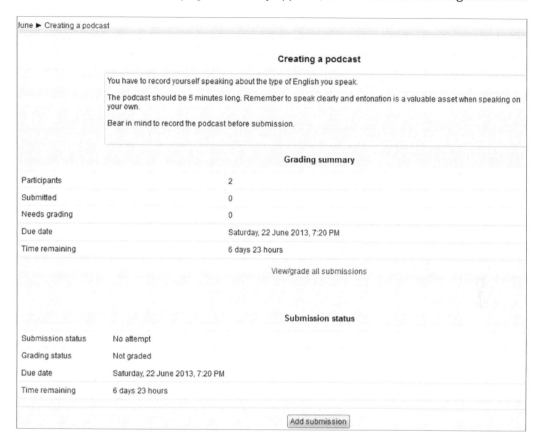

How it works...

When students have submitted their answers, we click on **View/grade all submissions** and see who did or did, not, submit their voice recording. We can see the file that they have uploaded in order to grade it; we click on it and we can listen to it using our default player. The files created by our students appear, as shown in the following screenshot:

6
Creating and Integrating Videos

In this chapter, we will cover the following recipes:

- ▶ Recording a video
- ▶ Uploading a video on YouTube
- ▶ Editing a video using a YouTube editor
- ▶ Embedding a Vimeo video
- ▶ Enhancing a video with comments
- ▶ Creating and embedding a Prezi presentation
- ▶ Creating a playlist
- ▶ Creating an animated video using Wideo

Introduction

This chapter explains how to create screencasts and edit them, as well as link and embed videos for our Moodle courses. The recipes use diverse free and open source multiplatform tools to record, edit, and convert different video files, covering the most common scenarios for multimedia Moodle activities.

It covers different ways to create and interact using either screencasts or videos. We will work with several multimedia assets, which will concern the baseline of a wildlife topic. This topic has many resources, which can be integrated with screencasts and videos available on the Web.

Creating screencasts using several types of free and open source software available on the Web is one of the main goals of this chapter. There is plenty of commercial software that can be used to create screencasts; however, we will not focus on them. We will also go through adding some special features to the screencasts in order to enhance them.

Videos can be recorded in several ways with several devices such as smartphones, tablets, iPads, and iPods among others. We are to focus on the way of creating and uploading them on a YouTube account and later to our Moodle course.

We can create a playlist in order to combine several videos and let our students watch them in a row. We do it by creating an account on the youtube.com website. The account is called channel. Our channel in YouTube can be either public or unlisted (only the people with the link can watch it); it depends on how we want to carry it out.

We can create some screencasts. Screencasts are the recordings from our screen. We can use them in order to present information to our students instead of showing presentations made using OpenOffice, PowerPoint, or Microsoft Word. Changing any of these into a screencast is more appealing to our students and not such a difficult task to carry out either.

When designing the screencast, we can create an explanation by recording our voice, so we will create a virtual board. We can choose to be visible to the audience or not. Another option is that our explanations can only be heard with no visualization of the teacher. This is quite an important aspect to be taken into account, especially in teaching because students need a dynamic explanation by their teacher.

We work with **Prezi** as well, which is a different way to present information. Another option is to choose an already designed Prezi and embed it in our Moodle course. There already are many Prezi slides easily available at prezi.com for us to get started. Let's dig into them!

Recording a video

In this recipe, we will record a video. We record a visit to the zoo by the sea because in this chapter, we deal with wildlife. Therefore, we may have a video from a visit to the zoo or any park that we might have once visited. Thus, in this instance, any smartphone or tablet among others is the most suitable option.

How to do it...

We will use a 720p HD video recorder. It is a video of a visit to a national park, where we can find several wild animals. Various players can be used in order to watch the video in our computer, but VLC media player is a very good option as it supports most video codecs. This software can be freely downloaded from the following website:

```
http://www.videolan.org/vlc/
```

VLC media player will allow us to watch the video that we have just recorded, as it supports all the common video recordings. Follow these steps to record a video and save it in our computer:

1. Record the video.

2. Connect the video recorder to the computer.

3. Scan the folder to open the files.

4. Select the video that you want to watch. Right-click on the video and then click on **Copy**.

5. Create a folder on your computer and paste the video on the folder that was created. The video to work with has been saved.

6. Using VLC media player, you can open the files that were saved in the computer. Click on **Media | Open File...**, as shown in the following screenshot:

7. Choose the file that you need to open.

8. Click on **Open**. The chosen video will now be played.

How it works...

We can upload the video that we have recorded to our Moodle course (there are some video formats that are not supported by Moodle). We can create a chat room in our Moodle course, to add some social interaction and let our students discuss the video among themselves, as well as the outing. Choose the section where we want to add this activity and follow these steps:

1. Click on **Add an activity or resource**.

2. Click on **Chat | Add**.

3. Complete the **Name of this chat room** and **Description** blocks.

4. Click on the **Show editing tools** link and select the **Insert Moodle media** icon. Navigate to **Find or upload a sound, video or applet ...** | **Upload a file** | **Browse....** Look for the file that you want to upload and click on it.

 You must take into account that there is a limitation on how much we can upload, so be careful with the size of the video to upload.

5. Navigate to **Open** | **Upload this file** | **Insert**.

6. Click on **Save and return to course**. It looks as shown in the following screenshot:

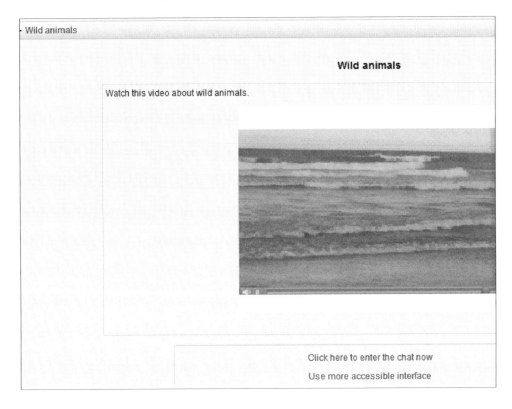

 It is important to point out that if the video is too long you may get a notification that it has exceeded the maximum size to be uploaded on Moodle, so it is always advisable to embed videos instead of uploading them on Moodle.

Uploading a video on YouTube

We can work with the video from the previous recipe and instead of uploading it on our Moodle course, we can upload it on YouTube. Before uploading the video, we first need to create an account in `youtube.com`.

Getting ready

We may have an account in `youtube.com`, but if we do not have one yet, we can create it very easily. So open the YouTube website. Click on **Sign in** on the top-right hand margin. Then click on the **CREATE AN ACCOUNT** icon and complete the necessary information in order to create the account.

How to do it...

After creating the account, we can start working on our YouTube channel. There are plenty of items that we can work with. YouTube seems to be a mixture of the most common social networks. We can add a picture of artwork and share our thoughts among any other features. Leaving these aside, we follow these steps to upload a video to this account:

1. Click on the name of your account and then click on **Video Manager**, as shown in the following screenshot:

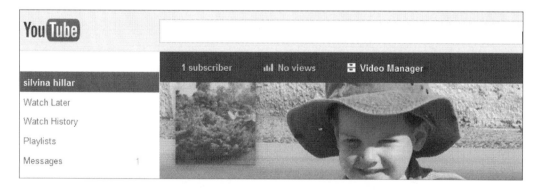

2. Click on **Upload | Select files to upload**, choose the file that you want to upload, and click on **Open**.

3. Within **Privacy settings**, you can choose among **Public**, **Private**, or **Unlisted**.

 Public means that all the people can watch it; **Private** means that only the owner of the channel can watch it; and **Unlisted** means that only the people with the link can watch it.

4. There are many other blocks that you can complete such as **Title**, **Description**, or **Tags**; it all depends on the way to use the video.

5. When the video is uploaded, it looks as shown in the following screenshot:

You will receive an automatic e-mail (noreply e-mail) telling you that the video is uploaded on your channel.

6. Click on the video.

7. Click on **Share** | **Embed** and copy the HTML code, as shown in the following screenshot:

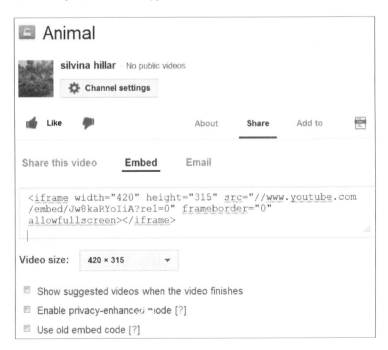

How it works...

Once the video is uploaded on the YouTube account we can embed it in our Moodle course; another option is to edit the video using the YouTube video editor, which is to be explored in the following recipe. We can also share the video using social networks. Let's embed the video in our Moodle course. Choose the weekly outline section where we would upload the resource and follow these steps:

1. Click on **Add an activity or resource**.

2. Click on **Label | Add**.

3. Complete the **Label text** block.

4. Click on **Show editing tools**, then on the **Edit HTML source** icon, and paste the code copied from the YouTube video.

5. Click on **Update**.

6. Click on **Save and return to course**; the resource looks as shown in the following screenshot:

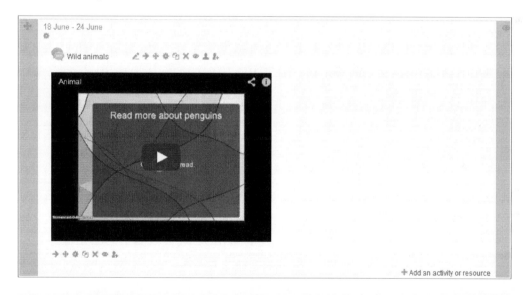

Editing a video using a YouTube editor

In this recipe we continue working with the YouTube website. There happens to be a video editor that has plenty of functions we can take advantage of. So, it is mandatory to have a YouTube account in order to use it.

Getting ready

We need to enter into our YouTube account in order to get ready to work with this recipe. We have to think what we want to do with our videos, taking into account that there are several ways that we can edit videos. We are to explore some options available at the time of writing. The advantage is that we can edit the video and use it after doing so. We can also combine the videos or use a piece of them.

How to do it...

After opening the YouTube website and signing into our account, we need to follow some steps in order to enter the video editor and start editing our video. We have to bear in mind what we want to do; in this instance, we will create a video out of the two videos and add music and captions. So, these are the steps that we have to follow:

1. Click on **Video Manager**.

2. You will see the videos that we have uploaded on our YouTube channel. Click on the video to edit.

3. Click on any of the icons beneath the video, such as **Enhancement**, as shown in the following screenshot:

4. Within **Enhancement**, we have the following options:

   □ **Auto-fix one-click fix for lighting and color**

   □ **Fine tune lighting and color**

   □ **Slow Motion**

   □ **Stabilize** (removes shaky camera options)

   Choose the option that you want to work with.

5. The screen of the video is divided in two halves; you can move the screen divider to see the **Original** and **Preview** options, as shown in the following screenshot:

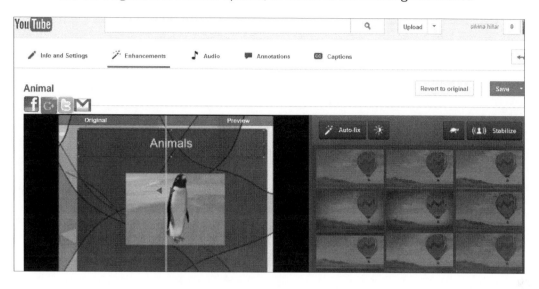

6. After choosing the **Enhancements** options, click on **Save**.

7. The edit will take some minutes and the video appears in the original version until the edit is processed.

8. Click on the video again.

9. Click on the **Annotations** icon.

10. Click on the down arrow next to **Add annotation**, as shown in the following screenshot:

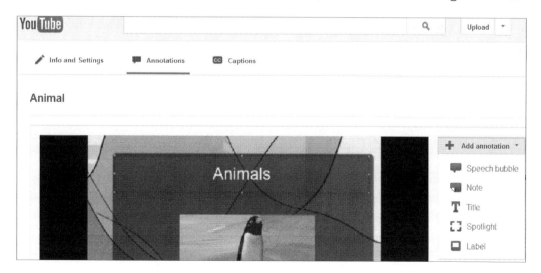

11. Click on **Note** to add annotations.

12. There appears a rectangle on the video where we can write the annotation.

13. There are several options to work with, as shown in the following screenshot:

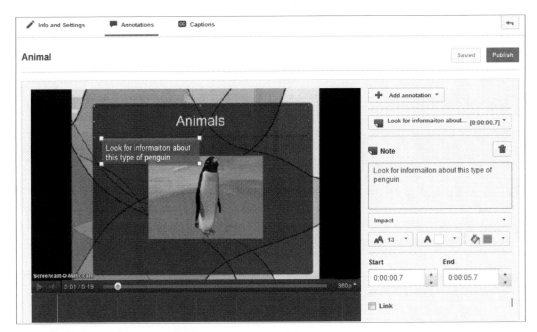

14. After writing the necessary annotations and editing them, click on **Publish** on the top-right hand side of the screen.

15. Click on **Captions** to add captions to the video.

    There is an option of having an automatic caption through voice recognition.

16. Click on **Add captions** and then select **Transcribe and sync** to synchronize the captions with the video, as shown in the following screenshot:

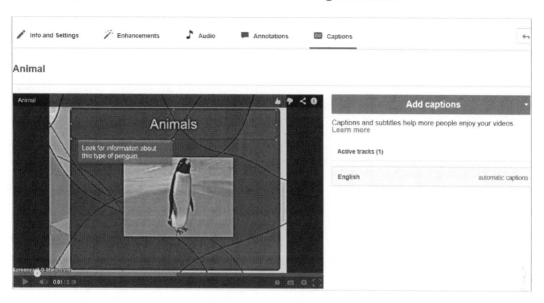

17. Save the changes.
18. Click on **Audio**.
19. Click on a track you want to add to the video and click on **Save**.

    It will take some time as the video edit is progressing.

How it works...

We can also use the YouTube video editor to continue editing our video. It allows us to combine the selected videos that we have uploaded on our account, photos, and videos with the Web. It is a tool that will allow us to create a resource that combines several resources. These are the steps to follow:

1. Click on the video to edit.
2. Click on any one of the icons below it, for example, **Enhancements**.
3. Click on **Try the YouTube Video Editor** on the bottom-right part of the margin.

4. Click on the video and drag it where it says **Drag videos here**, as shown in the following screenshot:

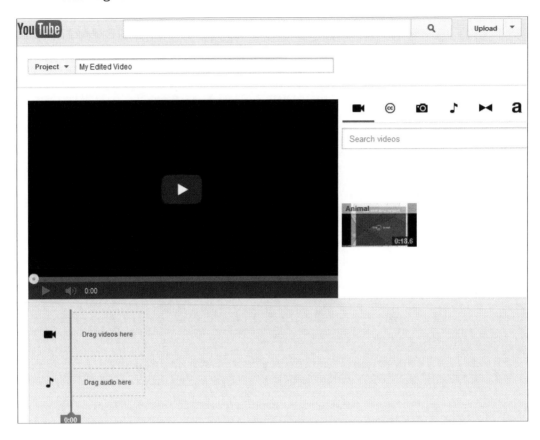

You can combine several videos using this editor.

5. Click on the **Creative Commons Videos** icon if you want to add any of the videos to the new project.

6. Click on the **Photos** icon to upload photos to the project.

7. After uploading the photo, drag it onto the project.

8. Click on the **Audio** icon and click on the desired file you want to add to the project, as shown in the following screenshot:

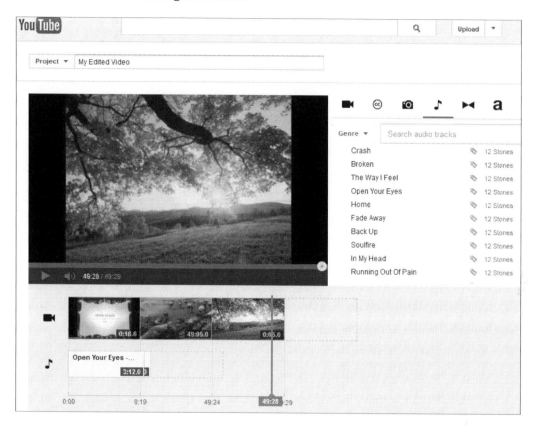

9. Click on the **Text** icon to add text.

10. Click on **Publish** when the project is ready.

   It will take some minutes for the video to be ready.

   When the video is ready, we can add a resource to our Moodle course.

Embedding a Vimeo video

We have been working with the YouTube website, but there are other websites, which are similar to it, and we can find different videos. One of the websites that offer similar services is Vimeo. It is either free or there are two paid options, as we can see on the website.

We can upload and store videos, watch and share videos by e-mail, URL, and social networks, or embed them. There is also an editor that allows us to enhance or add music to the videos. We can explore these options on the following website:

```
https://vimeo.com/
```

Getting ready

We need to create an account in order to start working with a Vimeo video, so we go to the just mentioned website. If we already have an account we sign in, or we join by completing the necessary information; alternatively, we just click on **Join with Facebook** (if we have an account in that social network), as shown in the following screenshot:

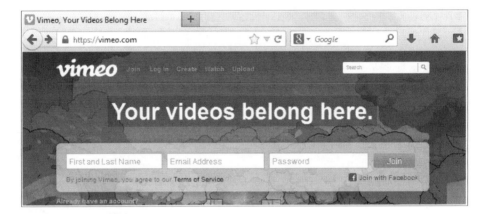

How to do it...

After signing in and entering into our account, we can upload videos in order to store them or we can look for videos to work with. If we want to use any existing video on the desired topic, look for them in the search block. In this recipe, we upload a video that we created. So, these are the steps that we have to follow:

1. Click on **Videos | My Videos**, as shown in the following screenshot:

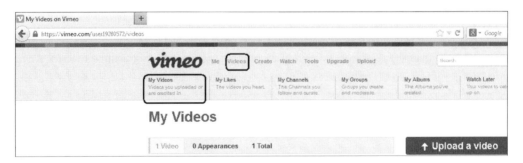

2. Click on **Upload a video**.

3. Click on **Choose a Video to Upload**.

4. Click on the video that you want to upload and click on **Open**.

5. Click on **Upload Selected Videos**, as shown in the following screenshot:

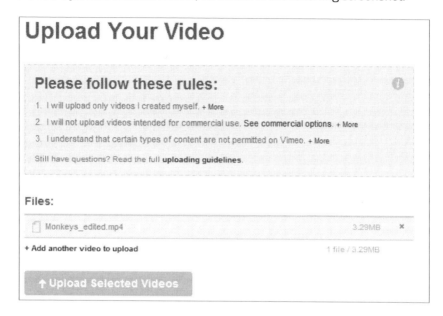

While the video is uploading, the following screenshot is shown:

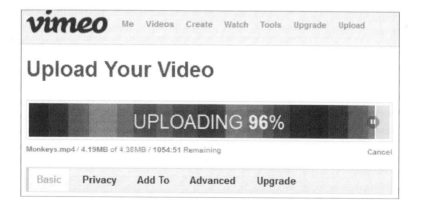

When the video has been uploaded, the following screenshot is shown:

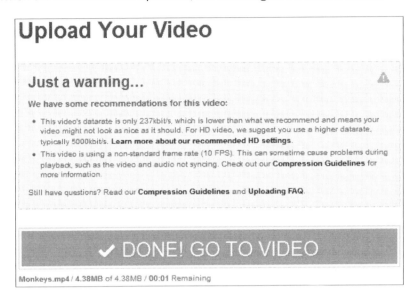

The video will be ready in some minutes; when it is ready, you will receive an e-mail.

How it works...

We have already uploaded a video on our Vimeo account. We can change the **Privacy** option within **Settings**, among other items. The **Privacy** option is important due to the fact that we can select who can use or watch our video for instance.

There is also a possibility to enhance our videos using the **Enhancer** icon. It helps us to make our videos more appealing, and they add some extra elements. It is similar to the YouTube editor but it is worth exploring it. Follow these steps to start editing the video:

1. Click on **Videos | My Videos**.
2. Click on **Settings** on the top-right hand side of the video to edit, as shown in the following screenshot:

3. Click on **Privacy** and choose the type of privacy. You should choose the **Anyone** option if you want to share the video in the Moodle course.

As regards to the type of privacy, these are the options available:

  ▸ **Anyone**: This option allows anybody to see the video
  ▸ **Only me**: This option makes the video private only to the owner of the channel
  ▸ **Only people I follow**: This option makes the video available to your Vimeo followers
  ▸ **Only people I choose**: This option allows the owner of the channel to select whom to show the video to
  ▸ **Only people with a password**: This option allows the owner of the channel to protect the video with a password and give it to the people he/she wants to share it with

4. Click on **Return to video**.

5. Click on **Create | Enhancer** within the upper ribbon.

6. Click on **Start Enhancing**, as shown in the following screenshot:

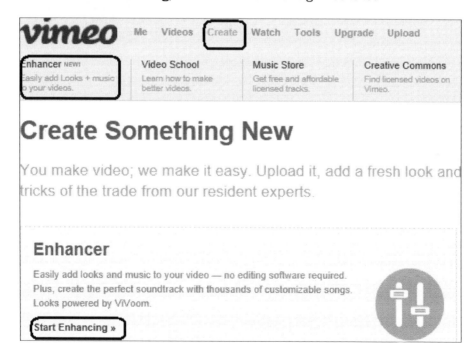

7. Click on **Start enhancing now**.

8. Click on the video to enhance.

9. Click on **Add a look**, choose the look, and click on **Enhance**, as shown in the following screenshot:

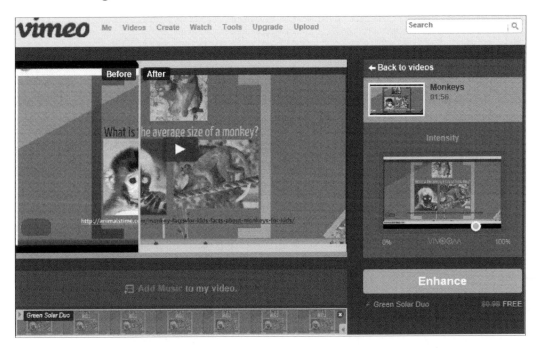

10. Click on **Save New Video**.

11. Choose the **Privacy** option of the new video and click on **Return to video**.

    The enhancement is in process. After some minutes, the video is ready.

12. Click on the video when it is ready.

13. Click on **Share** on the top-right hand margin of the video.

14. Copy the HTML code to embed the video in our Moodle course, as shown in the following screenshot:

Enhancing a video with comments

This recipe can be carried out using the YouTube Video Editor, which we have already explored in the *Uploading a video on YouTube* recipe, or we can use the https://www.wirewax. com/ website, which allows us to add comments to videos or tag people's faces.

Getting ready

First of all, we need to sign in, in order to create an account and start working with wireWAX. We also have the possibility to log in using Facebook. If we log in using Facebook, wireWAX helps you identify friends' faces in videos, as shown in the following screenshot:

How to do it...

After logging in to wireWAX, we can start editing our video. So, we need to look for a video to work with and think about the comments that we want to add. In this instance, as we are working with wild animals, we will not tag people's faces. Follow these steps:

1. At the bottom-left hand margin, there appears a block that reads **Click or drop your new video here...**; click on it to upload a file.

2. Below the block named in the preceding step, there is another one that reads **... or paste a video URL here...**.

3. Choose either step 1 or 2 to upload the video.

   The video is encoded and processed, so wait for some minutes.

4. Click on the video to start adding comments to it.

5. Click on the **+** sign on the top-left hand margin of the video to add a tag, as shown in the following screenshot:

6. Draw the desired geometrical shape using the pencil icon that appears on the video, as shown in the following screenshot:

7. Adjust the square.
8. Click on **+** to add the tag.
9. Click on the square to write a tag or a comment.
10. Click on the sidewards arrow.
11. Click on **+ build new pop-up**, as shown in the following screenshot:

12. Click on the arrow to adjust the square.

13. Click on **+** to add content to the square.

14. Click on the editor to change colors, as shown in the following screenshot:

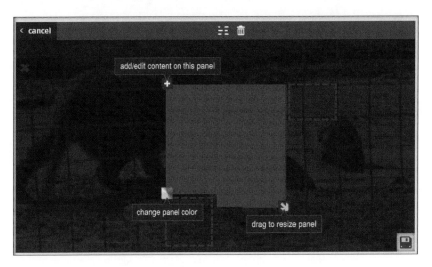

15. Click on **Save** to add the changes.

How it works...

There are more options that we can add to the annotations in the video. They can be explored using the **Help** button on the top-right margin of the video. There appear different settings beneath the video, which can be changed as desired by just clicking on the icons to the right.

When playing the video, we can read the annotations written in the video. They will be displayed as we have designed them. We can embed the video to our Moodle course by copying the embedding code, as shown in the following screenshot:

Creating and embedding a Prezi presentation

We can design a presentation using a cloud-based software, which is a zoomable canvas and explores ideas in a different way than the traditional one (such as the PowerPoint presentation). So, we can design a Prezi, which is a presentation, and we can embed it in our Moodle course. We need to go to `http://prezi.com/` to sign up and create an account.

Getting ready

We can sign up in the traditional way or by using Facebook, if you happen to have an account. There are three categories: **Public**, **Enjoy**, or **Pro**. In this recipe, we focus on the **Public** category, which is free of charge; the others are paid, but we can have a 30-day trial though.

How to do it...

After creating the account, we can start designing the Prezi presentation. The topic of this chapter is wild animals, so we can create a zoomable presentation of this topic. We are creating a resource for our Moodle course, so we can add plenty of information to our Prezi presentation. We have to follow these steps in order to design a Prezi presentation:

1. After signing up, we click on **New prezi**, as shown in the following screenshot:

2. The **Choose your template** window will appear; choose the desired template to start designing the Prezi presentation, as shown in the following screenshot:

3. Click on **Use Template**.

Templates are updated, so you may use one template and then you may not find it again, but new ones are to be available. Though, the steps remain the same.

4. Click on **Click to add Title** and write the title for your Prezi presentation.

5. Click on **Step 2** (click to zoom to this path point), which is at the left margin, as shown in the following screenshot:

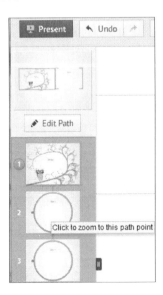

6. Edit **Step 2**. You can add a link to an official website of owls.

7. Click on **Step 3** to edit it. You can paste the URL of any video, related to owls.

8. Click on **Step 4** to edit. You can paste a short poem on owls.

9. When you finish editing the Prezi presentation, click on the **Save** icon though it is automatically saved.

10. Click on **Insert | Add Background Music...**, as shown in the following screenshot:

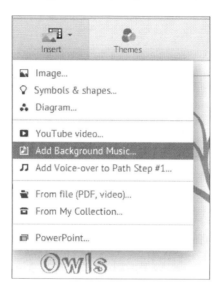

11. Choose the file you want to upload and click on **Open**.

12. Click on **Share | Online presentation**, as shown in the following screenshot:

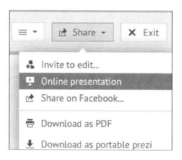

13. Click on **Copy link**.

How it works...

We have just designed our prezi. We worked with the basic features; we can explore it even deeper in order to enhance it. It is a different way to present attractive resources to students. Now, it is time to upload the Prezi presentation on our Moodle course. These are the steps that we have to follow:

1. Click on **Add an activity or resource**.

2. Click on **URL | Add**.

3. Complete the **Name** and **Description** blocks.

4. Paste the link copied from the Prezi presentation within the **External URL** block, which is within **Content**.

5. Click on **Save and display**; the resource looks as shown in the following screenshot:

Creating a playlist

We can create a playlist, so that instead of showing one video to our students, we can show them several videos. In order to create a playlist, we are going to use a YouTube account. As we have already used this website in previous recipes, we already have one; thus, we just need to log in and start working.

Getting ready

We have to think of the videos to work with before creating the playlist. In this chapter, we work with wild animals, so we can look for some videos that we have already worked with. We should create a playlist about a certain topic so that each video adds more elements to the previous one.

How to do it...

We enter our YouTube channel after logging in where we have to look for videos to create the playlist. Then, we need to follow the ensuing steps in order to design it:

1. Click on **Video Manager** at the upper ribbon.
2. Click on **Playlists** on the left-hand side margin.
3. Click on **+ New playlist** on the right-hand side margin.
4. Complete the **Playlist title** and **Playlist description** blocks.
5. Click on **Create playlist**, as shown in the following screenshot:

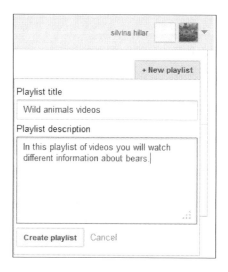

6. Click on **Add video by URL**. Choose a video and copy its URL.
7. Paste the URL of the video you want to work with in the block and click on **Add**.
8. Repeat steps 6 and 7 as many times as the number of videos you want to add to the playlist.
9. When the playlist is ready, click on **Done**, as shown in the following screenshot:

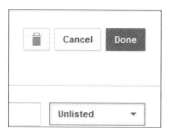

10. Click on **Share | Embed** and copy the HTML code, as shown in the following screenshot:

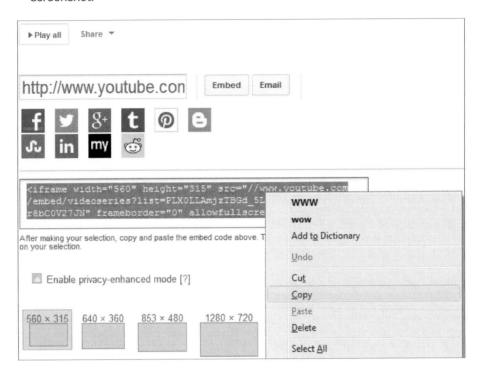

How it works...

We have already created a playlist in the youtube.com website. We can embed the playlist in our Moodle course as a resource of bears. We can look for videos of different topics or we can even create videos, upload them to our channel, and create a playlist using them.

We can embed the playlist in our Moodle course. We would like our students to watch the videos in a row. In order to design this type of resource, we have to copy the embedding code for the playlist. We enter the Moodle course and choose the weekly outline section where we want to upload the resource and follow these steps:

1. Click on **Add an activity or resource**.
2. Click on **Page | Add**.
3. Complete the **Name** and **Description** blocks.
4. Click on the **Edit HTML source** icon within the **Page content** block.
5. Paste the HTML code copied from the YouTube website.
6. Click on **Update**.

7. Click on **Save and display**; the playlist appears, as shown in the following screenshot:

Creating an animated video using Wideo

We can create animated videos using Wideo, which is an online animation platform that lets us create, edit, and share videos for free. Wideo is a website through which we can either use the images within the platform or upload them on our own. We can also add animation and videos in order to create a new one. It is another interesting way to create a resource for students.

Getting ready

First of all, go to `http://wideo.co/`. We have to sign up in order to start creating videos. We can also use the videos created by others. In this instance, we design a simple video to upload in our Moodle course.

How to do it...

After signing up and creating our account, we have to think about the topic of our video. In this instance, we continue working with wild animals; we are to focus on sea animals this time. We have to follow these steps to start creating our video:

1. Click on **Create a new wideo**.

2. Click on the **Background** icon and select **Images**.

3. Choose the image you want to insert as the background, as shown in the following screenshot:

4. Navigate to **Objects | My stuff | Upload | Select file**, click on the file to upload, and then click on **Open**.

5. Click on **Ok** after reading the necessary information.

6. Click on the image uploaded and click on **Animate**, as shown in the following screenshot:

7. Choose the desired animation.

8. Click on **Add** to add another scene, as shown in the following screenshot:

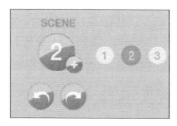

9. Repeat steps 2 up to 6 as many times as needed.

10. Navigate to **Sound | UPLOAD YOUR OWN SOUNDS** or choose any of the available sounds.

11. Click on **Save**.

How it works...

There are plenty of features to explore in Wideo; we have just designed a simple animated video to design a resource for students. After creating the video and saving it, we can paste the embedding code to our Moodle course. These are the steps that we have to follow:

1. Click on **User profile**, as shown in the following screenshot:

2. Click on **My wideos**.

3. Click on the icon, as shown in the following screenshot:

4. Click on **Share**.

5. There appears a pop-up window showing the embedding code. Copy it in order to paste it onto our Moodle course.

   There are also other ways in which you can share the wideo.

6. We can create a resource in our Moodle course, such as a page activity, and we can see the video that we have created in Wideo, as shown in the following screenshot:

7
Working with Bitmaps and Photographs

In this chapter, we will cover the following recipes:

- ▸ Selecting between lossy and lossless compression schemes
- ▸ Resizing photos to their appropriate size
- ▸ Adding hotspots to photos
- ▸ Editing color curves
- ▸ Adding effects and applying filters
- ▸ Uploading images to Moodle
- ▸ Creating animated 3D graphics
- ▸ Linking external image files from thinglink.com
- ▸ Embedding images from thinglink.com

Introduction

A bitmap graphic is made up of a grid with a lot of little squares (pixels). In each pixel we put a different color; adding color to the pixels, we build an image pixel by pixel. As we move backwards from the grid, the pixels blend and we can see a photographic image, a bitmap.

This chapter explains how to work with different types of bitmap image file formats that use lossy and lossless compression schemes. The recipes use diverse tools to edit, enhance, and convert the different image files, covering most scenarios for multimedia Moodle activities, which deals with art and photographs as the baseline topic.

Animated graphics are a very important asset to take into account if we want to enhance the look of our Moodle course. We learn how to create them and insert them in Moodle.

Adding elements to the graphics is also an interesting point to take into account when designing an appealing course. We learn how to add hotspots and effects to photos and apply filters.

After reading this chapter, we will learn how to link, edit, and embed bitmaps and photographs. We will also be able to resize and convert them to the most appropriate formats for Moodle courses. The recipes are designed in such a way that they are all combined.

When thinking of art or photography, we may have in mind the idea of a painter or a photographer, though people who work for these fields may have related jobs, such as taking pictures for magazines. The idea is to deal with these topics as a general knowledge baseline and promote the use of photographs or pictures in order to create engaging activities in our Moodle course.

We can also create social interaction among students using images and photographs. We are going to learn the best way to upload them to our Moodle course according to what we want to design. Moreover, we can also design activities in which we use famous works of art of well-known painters from different times in order to broaden the culture of our students. In addition, we could interact with a history or an art teacher, develop the understanding of a painting or picture taken at a certain time, and explore the history of the said period.

Selecting between lossy and lossless compression schemes

When we save a bitmap image, we can choose between lossy and lossless compression schemes to reduce the file size that stores the color information for each pixel that composes the bitmap.

Lossless compression schemes retain all the original color information; therefore, they keep the original quality but produce a large file size. On the other hand, lossy compression schemes replace some color information with approximated values to produce a smaller file size. Thus, lossy compression schemes don't keep the original quality.

In this recipe, we will learn how to choose between one scheme over the other—the smaller size is not the only thing that matters.

Getting ready

We are going to capture an image of the map of the Louvre Museum in France in order to use it in our Moodle course. Here, we contrast both lossy and lossless compression schemes with this map. We save them as .png not as .jpg because the resolution is low, and it is not convenient to work with .jpg.

How to do it...

Go to `http://maps.google.com/` and capture the image of the location of the Louvre Museum in France. We have already covered maps in *Chapter 2, Working with 2D and 3D Maps*. We are going to use GIMP to paste the capture of the image.

We can download and install GIMP 2.6.8 from the website `http://www.gimp.org/downloads/`. After installing and running GIMP, these are the steps that we have to follow:

1. Go to `http://maps.google.com/`.

2. Look for the location of the Louvre Museum in France.

3. Press the *Prt Scr* key when you find the location of the museum.

4. Run the GIMP software.

5. Paste the image in GIMP.

6. Click on **Rectangle Select Tool: Select a rectangular region R** and choose the part of the map where the museum is located, as shown in the following screenshot:

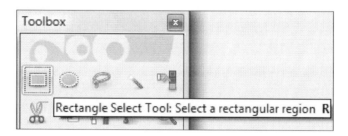

7. Click on **Edit | Cut**.

8. Click on **File | New | OK** and paste the new image in the new document.

9. Repeat the preceding step because you are going to work with two files, saving them in two different formats.

How it works...

We are going to compare both the files. The image is the same, that is, the part of the map that shows the location of the Louvre Museum in France. What we change is the format, that is, the type of the image file. The PNG format only uses lossless compression.

Remember that we are still working with GIMP. Follow these steps in order to compare both the images:

1. Click on **File | Save as ...**.

2. Complete the **Name** field by typing `Louvre_Lossy`.

3. Click on the down arrow in **All images** at the bottom of the pop-up window and choose **JPEG image**, as shown in the following screenshot:

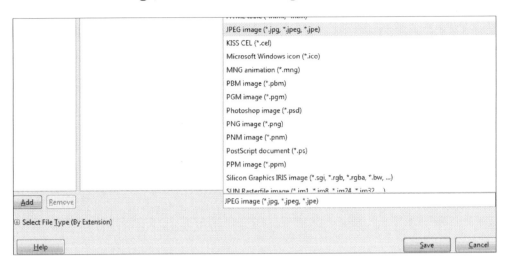

4. Click on **Select File Type (By Extension)** and choose **JPEG**.

5. Click on **Save**.

6. The image is blurry and pixelated. If you see them in color, they tend to fade away. When you enlarge the `.jpg` image, you will notice that it increases the blur. Pixels with different colors that add noise to the image delete the color information and replace it with pixels of approximated values. This is shown in the following screenshot:

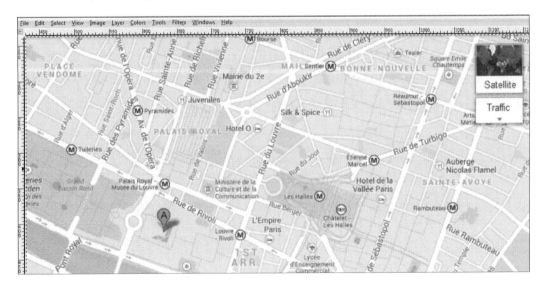

7. It is time to see how `.png` works. This type of image is a lossless compression. Follow steps 1 to 5; the difference is that in the **Name** field, you type `Louvre_Lossless` and make sure the format is **PNG image** (steps 3 and 4).

8. The image will be clearer and of better quality than the previous one. It is shown in the following screenshot:

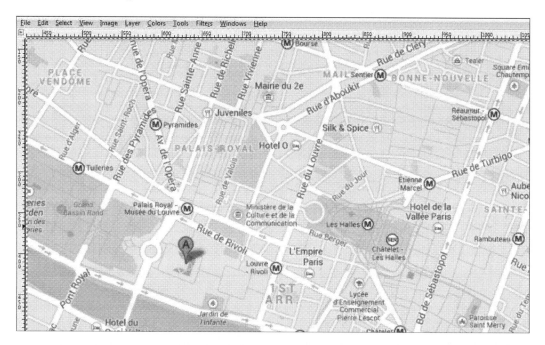

Resizing photos to their appropriate size

When working with pictures taken by digital cameras, smartphones, or tablets, we usually have different dimensions on the screen. Your Moodle course displays data on the web browser, and the web browser usually does not take advantage of the whole screen size. Technology offers devices with different screens; therefore, we have to consider them when dealing with mobile and special devices.

Getting ready

As previously mentioned, there are different screen sizes so the target will be different. The full HD is of 1920 x 1080; it does not fit all the devices though, so we are going to work with the following size: 1000 x width and 700 x height as the maximum size of the images.

How to do it...

It is typical that pictures usually have more than 3000 pixels in width and 2400 pixels in height. We do not want to upload such a huge image to our Moodle course, so we need to resize the photograph with the appropriate height and width values. The larger the image dimensions are, the larger the file sizes would be. We are going to work with GIMP in this recipe. Therefore, follow these steps in order to resize the image:

1. Click on **File | Open...** and browse for the picture to work with.

2. Click on **File | Save a Copy...** to keep the original file untouched.

3. Write a name for the image and click on **Save** twice.

4. Click on **Image | Scale Image...**, as shown in the following screenshot:

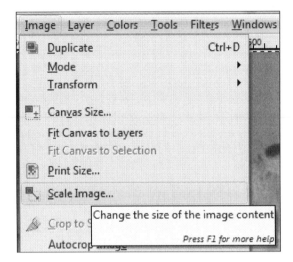

 Scaling the image changes the ratio. The aspect ratio is the proportion between the width and height. It is the same image with fewer pixels (downscaling).

5. Write 1000 in **Width** within **Image Size**, and **Height** will automatically change to **750**; the aspect ratio is calculated automatically.

6. Click on **Scale**, as shown in the following screenshot:

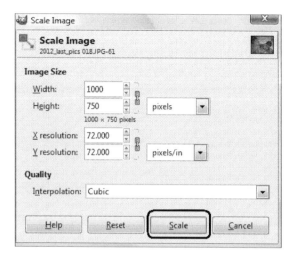

How it works...

We have resized the image, and the result of the new resolution 1000 x 750 pixels. If you want a full screen image, check how it looks when you upload it to the Moodle course. You have to save the new image, which is resized, in order to be able to upload it on our Moodle course. Therefore, click on **File | Save**. Remember that we have saved a copy of the original image previously. The image looks as shown in the following screenshot:

Adding hotspots to photos

In this recipe, we work with photos and add hotspots to them. Hotspots are hyperlinks to the photos, so we can enrich a photo with additional content. There are options to add hotspots to images; one of them is to use a website such as `http://www.imagespike.com/interactive-image-builder.html`, follow the steps, and get the HTML code, or link, to embed it in our Moodle course. Another option is to use GIMP in order to create them, so the second option is the one that we will explore in this recipe.

Getting ready

We have to choose a photo and think of links that we want to add to it. A good idea related to art is to choose some famous paintings and add hotspots related to the painter who did them and his/her biography.

Since there are many social networks available for us today, hotspots can be added using them. We can add the URL of different networks related to a photo or a specific subject. The photo is linked when clicked on the hotspot.

How to do it...

It is good advice to resize the image before we add hotspots to it, especially if we are dealing with a photo. We then need to run GIMP and follow these steps in order to add hotspots to the image:

1. Click on **File | Open...**. Choose the photo to work with.

2. Click on **Filters | Web | Image Map...**. The editor block appears, and we can add the hotspots.

3. Click on the left-hand margin to choose a shape to map the image, as shown in the following screenshot:

4. Circle a part of the image to add hotspots.

5. Another pop-up window appears. Uncheck the **Relative link** checkbox.

6. Complete the blocks marked with the link that you want to display, as shown in the following screenshot:

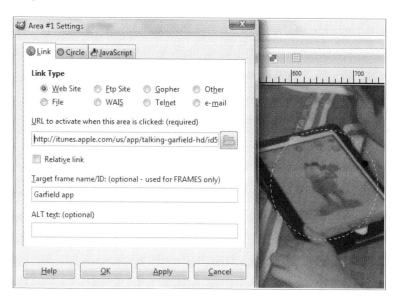

7. Click on **Apply | OK**.

8. The links appear on the right panel.

9. Save the file as `.map`. Click on **File | Save** and the `.map` extension will appear automatically. Click on **Save**.

10. You can add as many hotspots to the photo as you want; if so, repeat steps 2 to 7 as many times as the number of hotspots you want to add.

11. When you finish adding hotspots, click on **File | Save**.

12. Click on **View | Source**. A pop-up window displaying the HTML code will appear, as shown in the following screenshot:

How it works...

We have just added hotspots to the photo. Our photo will not be an ordinary one; when hovering the mouse over the selected area, we will be able to click and the website that we have selected will appear.

It is time to upload the image to our Moodle course. Therefore, choose the weekly outline section where you want to add it; we can then upload the image to the **Summary** section. These are the steps that we have to follow:

1. Click on the **Edit summary** icon in the weekly section that you want to upload the image.

2. If you want to complete the **Section name** block, uncheck the **Use default section name** checkbox.

3. In the **Summary** block, click on the **Insert/edit image** icon.

4. Navigate to **Find or upload an image | Upload a file | Browse** and look for the photo that you want to upload.

5. Click on **Upload this file**.

6. Complete the **Image description** block. Click on **Insert**.

7. Click on the **HTML** icon.

8. This is the original HTML code you will see:

```
<p><img
src="http://localhost/draftfile.php/5/user/draft/317291260/
Garfield_iPads.JPG" alt="iPad_Garfield_app" height="750"
width="1000" />
</p>
```

9. Insert the following code before />:

```
usemap="#map" border="0"
```

10. The code will read as follows:

```
<p>
    <img
src="http://localhost/draftfile.php/5/user/draft/317291260/
Garfield_iPads.JPG" alt="iPad_Garfield_app" height="750"
width="1000" usemap="#map" border="0"/>
</p>
```

11. Now, insert a new line after the last line and paste the code from GIMP's map source:

```
<p> <img src="http://localhost/draftfile.php/5/user/
draft/317291260/Garfield_iPads.JPG" alt="iPad_Garfield_app"
height="750" width="1000" usemap="#map" border="0"/>
</p>
<map name="map">
<!-- #$-:Image map file created by GIMP Image Map plug-in -->
<!-- #$-:GIMP Image Map plug-in by Maurits Rijk -->
<!-- #$-:Please do not edit lines starting with "#$" -->
<!-- #$VERSION:2.3 -->
<!-- #$AUTHOR:Silvina -->
<area shape="circle" coords="654,509,87" target="Garfield app"
href="http://itunes.apple.com/us/app/talking-garfield-hd/
id555937407?mt=8" />
</map>
```

12. Do not copy the code of the image because you have already uploaded the image into our Moodle course. It was the first step! The final code is:

```
<p> <img
src="http://localhost/draftfile.php/5/user/draft/484863281/
Garfield_iPads.JPG" alt="iPad_Garfield_app" usemap="#map"
height="750" border="0" width="1000" />
</p>
<p>
```

```
<map name="map"> <!-- #$-:Image map file created by GIMP
Image Map plug-in --> <!-- #$-:GIMP Image Map plug-in
by Maurits Rijk --> <!-- #$-:Please do not edit lines
starting with "#$" --> <!-- #$VERSION:2.3 -->
<!-- #$AUTHOR:Silvina -->
   <area shape="circle" coords="654,509,87" target="Garfield
app" href="http://itunes.apple.com/us/app/talking-garfield-hd/
id555937407?mt=8" />
   </map>
</p>
```

13. Click on **Update**, as shown in the following screenshot:

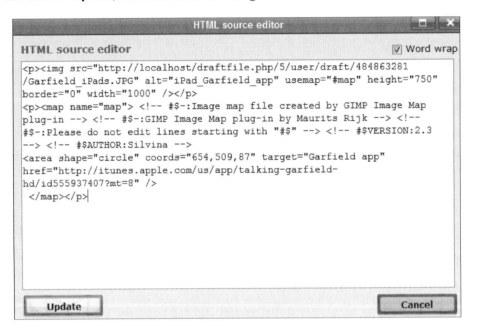

14. Click on **Save changes**.

When hovering the mouse over the image, you will be able to click on the selected image and the website that we have linked to, and it will appear.

Editing color curves

We can change the color in our pictures by editing color curves. Since we are dealing with art, it would be a good idea to work with the art of your students or with a well-known painting as well; for example, to add lightness or darkness to a picture in order to change the perceived time of day. We are going to work with GIMP, which we have already used in the previous recipes.

Getting ready

We have to choose a photo or a painting for which we want to change its color. We add a bit of our art in order to alter the image. It is a very simple recipe. So, let's see how to do it.

How to do it...

After choosing the photo or painting, we run GIMP. We can add this type of effect to our photos when we want to deal with a specific topic. We can also use it for prewriting activities by adding different colors so that students' perceptions are different.

Color is an essential element that can give a special condiment to students' homework. Follow these steps in order to edit color curves:

1. Click on **File | Open...** and browse for the picture to work with.
2. Click on **Colors | Curves...**.
3. A pop-up window appears displaying the curves that you can change.
4. Move the linear histogram to make the image darker or lighter.
5. You can also work with individual channels, say, adding a value to increase the intensity of one of the colors as shown in the following screenshot:

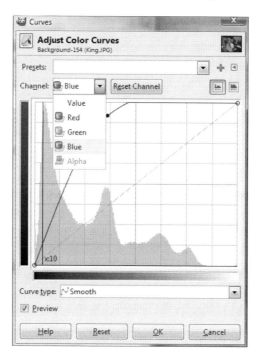

6. You can add the blue value because the picture is of a party. To do so, click on the down arrow in **Value| Blue**.

7. When you have finished adjusting color curves, click on **OK**.

8. Save the changes to the photo. Click on **File | Save | Save**.

How it works...

It is time to see how these curves work on a photo. To do so, we compare the same photo before and after adjusting color curves to it. The following screenshot spots the differences in color. The graph on the right-hand margin shows how we applied the color curve:

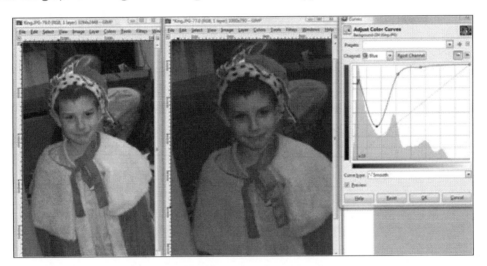

Adding effects and applying filters

In this recipe, we continue working with GIMP software, which has already been used in previous recipes in this chapter. We apply different effects and filters to the photographs. We can also work with paintings from our own students or famous painters as well. Though, here, we continue working with photos.

Getting ready

First of all, we have to choose the pictures that we want to work with. They can be personal pictures, as the ones that I chose previously; alternatively, we can work with photos from the Internet, but we have to bear in mind copyright issues. Let's change our photos.

How to do it...

We are going to run the GIMP software and choose a photo to work in our Moodle course afterwards. The effects that we could apply depend on the type of activity to be designed. These are the steps that we have to follow:

1. Open the file that you are going to work with. Click on **File | Open** and browse for the photo.

2. Click on **File | Save a copy... | Save**.

3. Click on **Filters | Artistic | Cartoon...**, as shown in the following screenshot:

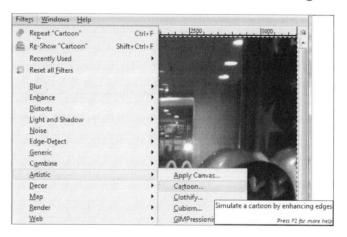

4. There appears the **Cartoon** pop-up window.

5. Choose the **Mask radius** and **Percent black** values, as shown in the following screenshot:

6. The **Preview** checkbox is ticked in the previous screenshot; therefore, if you click on the four-points arrow, you have the preview of the cartooned photo.

7. When you agree with the changes, click on **OK**.

8. Now, the photo has the appearance of a cartoon. Save the file. Navigate to **File | Save | Save**.

How it works...

We are going to compare both the photos before and after applying the cartoon effect. We have worked with a picture of a boy. He is the same boy from the previous recipes; we can design a writing activity with these photos. It would also be a great idea to work with a picture of scenery and apply other effects. So, let's compare the photo as it was before and after applying the effect. The screenshot to the left shows the photo and the one to the right the cartoon:

There's more

We can also apply other effects to the photos. For example, we can add the photocopy effect, change a new picture into an old photo, or combine a film strip. Exploring GIMP alternatives as regards to the changes that we can apply to a photo can take a whole chapter of the book, but this is not the aim. The appropriate effect should be selected in relation to the design and/or the aim of each activity. Let's explore one more alternative.

Applying old photo effect to a photo

We are going to work with the old photo effect. Here, we are going to work with a picture of two little children. Follow these steps:

1. Navigate to **File | Open...**, and browse for the picture that you want to work with.

2. Save the photo with a new name. Navigate to **File | Save as...**, and write a new name for the photo.

3. Navigate to **Filters | Decor | Old Photo...**, as shown in the following screenshot:

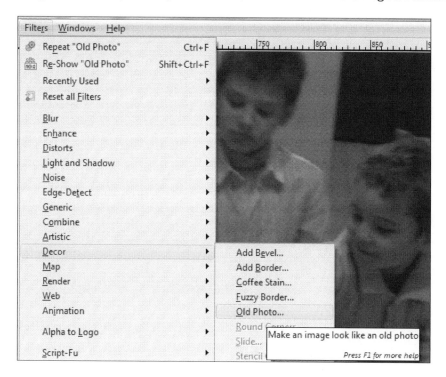

4. There will appear a pop-up window, and you may add changes to the way you want the photo effect, as shown in the following screenshot:

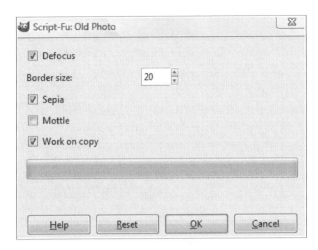

5. Click on **OK**. The following screenshot shows the same photo as it was before to the left and later with changes to the right:

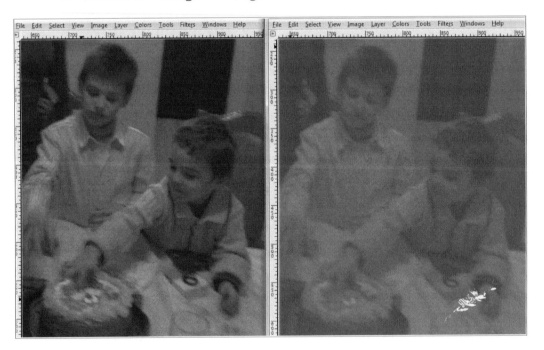

Uploading images to Moodle

In the previous recipes, we have worked with different types of images, but we have not designed activities with them. The aim of this chapter is to work with images and photographs, so it is time to upload them into our Moodle course.

Getting ready

We are working with art and photographs in this chapter, so we have to design an activity to cope with the previous bitmaps and photographs. We add a map of the Louvre Museum to an HTML block in the Moodle course.

We have saved the same image in both formats: .png and .jpg. We will insert .png in our Moodle course because we have already learned the difference in quality. When hovering the mouse over the said image, we can click and enter the official website of the Louvre Museum because we are linking the said image with a website.

How to do it...

We are going to enter our Moodle course and follow these steps:

1. Click on the down arrow in **Add...** within the block of **Add a block**.

2. Choose **HTML**, as shown in the following screenshot:

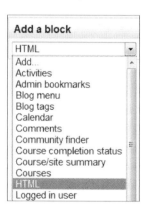

3. When the new block appears, click on the **Configure** icon (the gears icon).

4. Complete the **Block title** field.

5. In the **Content** block, click on the **Insert/edit image** icon and navigate to **Find or upload an image | Upload a file | Browse**.

6. Choose the .png file.

7. Select the image and navigate to **Open | Upload this file**.

8. Complete the **Image description** block.

9. Click on **Appearance**.

10. Click on the down arrow in **Alignment** and choose **Middle**.

11. Within **Dimensions**, type 200. The **Constrain proportions** block is ticked so the aspect radio is kept.

12. Click on **Insert**.

13. Click on the image and click on the **Insert/edit link** icon, as shown in the following screenshot:

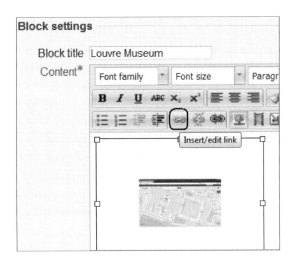

14. Complete the information in the pop-up window and create a link to the website http://www.louvre.fr/llv/commun/home.jsp?bmLocale=en.

15. Click on **Insert**.

16. Click on **Save changes**.

How it works...

We have just uploaded the image of the Louvre Museum that we created in our Moodle course. We did not upload it in the ordinary way; we have created a link to a website using the said image. It is an another way to add hotspots; the only difference is that we can add only one link. The other way we learned to do it is through using different sections of the images.

Therefore, when hovering the mouse over the said image, it will look as shown in the following screenshot:

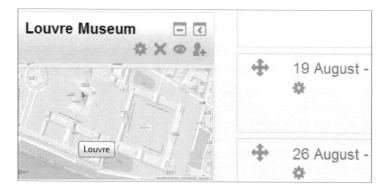

We can also upload image files in the ordinary way without creating links to a website, and it would sometimes be more attractive for our students to do it by themselves. Instead of creating an ordinary link with words, an icon related to something that they are going to deal with is a good idea to strengthen our Moodle course.

Creating animated 3D graphics

We are going to create animated 3D graphics in order to make our course more appealing. We can create different types of animations according to the activity that we want to design. We can use 3D images from http://sketchup.google.com/3dwarehouse/, or we can create them using Google Maps in 3D satellite view.

Considering the fact that we are dealing with art and photographs, we can create an animated GIF going from Sausalito, CA to SFMOMA in San Francisco. To go from one place to the other, we need to cross the Golden Gate Bridge, which is fascinating in 3D. We can try different destinations trying to spot out 3D views like this one.

Getting ready

We can design animated graphics using tools available online or via free and open source software.

In this recipe, we take captured images from Google Maps, and we create an animated gif using them. We need to take some of them in order to create the animation. We can also take images in order to design another type of activity.

How to do it...

We need to enter Google Maps and get directions in order to get the 3D images. We have already dealt with maps in *Chapter 2, Working with 2D and 3D Maps*, so we are using the website and clicking on some options in order to get the images. Follow these steps:

1. Go to `https://maps.google.com/`.

2. Complete the **Get directions** blocks with the desired directions.

3. Click on **GET DIRECTIONS**.

4. Click on **Satellite** to the right.

5. Click on **3D** to the left under **GET DIRECTIONS** (you can choose between **2D** or **3D**).

6. It looks as shown in the following screenshot:

7. Follow the direction and press the *Prt Scr* key to capture some images.

8. Save the images in GIMP as JPEG.

How it works...

In this recipe, we are going to work with a website that creates an animated gif image. We work with photographs showing different sceneries taken from Google Maps. After selecting the images or photographs to upload, follow these steps to create the animated graphics:

1. Go to `http://picasion.com/`.

2. Click on **Choose file** and choose the image that you want to upload.

3. Repeat step 2 as many times as necessary. To add more images, click on **Add one more picture** as many times as required, as shown in the following screenshot:

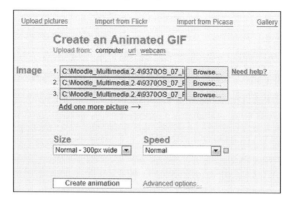

4. Choose the size of the animated graphic, and click on the down arrow in the **Size** block.

5. Choose the speed of the animated graphic, and click on the down arrow in the **Speed** block.

6. Click on **Create animation**.

7. The animated graphic that you have just created is displayed.

8. We can copy the **HTML code for blog/website code** in order to embed it or click on **Save this animation to your computer**, as shown in the following screenshot:

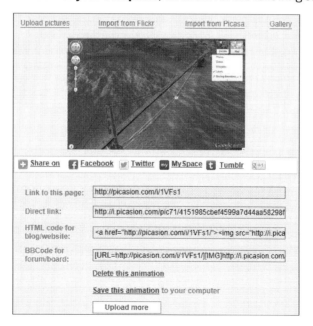

We have just created some animated graphics using Google Maps; now we can add an activity to our Moodle course. It would be suitable to add the GIF image to the description of the activity and add the link to the map so that students can enjoy the view. Besides, we need to point out where we took the images from.

Linking external image files from thinglink.com

This is a very spicy recipe. We are going to work with external files added to a photo using `http://www.thinglink.com/`. We can "create rich images with music, video, sound, text & more", as stated on the website. It is very useful as a resource introducing a new topic.

Teaching is enhanced when a visual aid is provided to our students, no matter which subject we are teaching. It is sometimes very difficult to have photos of all the things that we want to show them; we are going to work on it so we can find them easily in Flickr (`http://www.flickr.com/`). If we happen to have a wide collection of pictures, we can use one of them.

Getting ready

Using Flickr to search for photos is an amazing tool, due to the fact that we can insert them in our Moodle course in several ways. We can copy the link of the file, or we can embed it using the HTML code. Another option is to enable it through our **File picker** window; here, we need to switch our role to an administrator.

 We always have to look for the copyright of each photo to check whether it is public or not.

We can also download a photo from Flickr if it is allowed and work with it. Another option is to work with images of our own, which is the option that we are choosing. So, let's see how to do it.

How to do it...

First of all, we need to think beforehand which photo to use and the possible links that we are to deal with. As was stated before, we have options where to take photos from. Here, we use a personal photo of a boy in the lab.

The second step to take into consideration is the links that we can add to the image. As it is the picture of a boy in the lab, we can add external links of websites, science videos, podcasts which could have been created by students, and music among other possibilities. So, we have to think of them.

Now, go to `http://www.thinglink.com/` and create a free account. We need to follow these steps:

1. Click on **JOIN NOW!**.

2. You can log in using either a Facebook or Twitter account. Another option is to sign up on thinglink.com completing the necessary blocks.

3. Click on **SIGN UP FOR FREE!**.

4. Click on **GO TO YOUR STREAM**.

5. Click on **CREATE** on the top-right hand margin.

6. Import an image to work with, and click on **Choose images**. There are other ways to upload images using Facebook, Flickr, or the Web, as shown in the following screenshot:

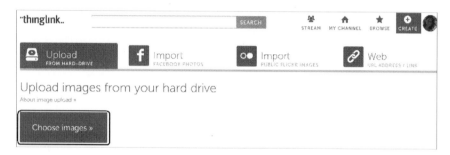

7. Click on the photo to work with.

8. Click on **Open**.

9. Complete the **TITLE** block.

10. Click on the photo to add a tag, as shown in the following screenshot:

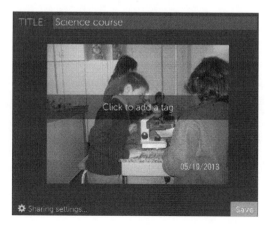

11. There appears a square.

12. Move the geometrical figure and adjust it in the microscope.

13. Open a new tab and look for the definition of microscope in Wikipedia, http://www.wikipedia.org/.

14. Copy the URL.

15. Paste the URL in the **Link** block.

16. Complete the **Description** block, as shown in the following screenshot:

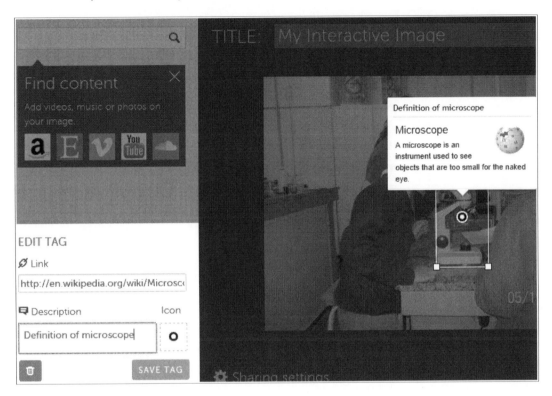

17. Click on **SAVE TAG**.

18. Click on the photo to add another tag. You can upload an album or a photo from your Facebook or Flickr page, if they are public.

19. Copy the URL of the album or the photo and paste it on the **Link** block.

20. Complete the **Description** block.

21. Click on the **Icon** block and choose the Facebook icon (if you uploaded a photo or album from the said network), as shown in the following screenshot:

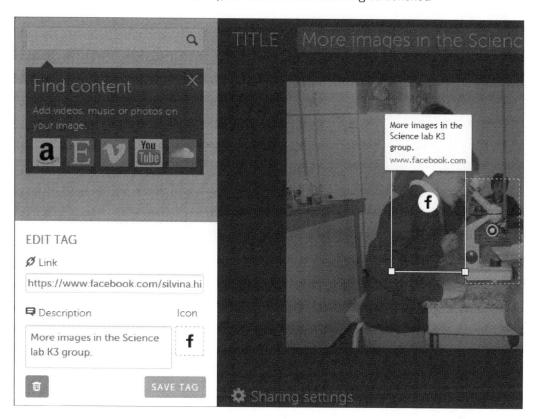

22. Click on **SAVE TAG**.

23. Repeat steps 18 to 22 to upload more content to the photo.

24. When it is ready, click on **SAVE** on the right-hand side of the image.

 We can click on the icons that appear on the left-hand side, such as YouTube, and complete the search block to look for content related to the image. It is advisable to look at it beforehand.

How it works...

The photo has got icons on it. When we hover the mouse over the photo, we can see the bubbles that predict what the links are about. Here, we have added more images from a public Facebook account, the definition of a microscope, a YouTube video showing an experiment, and a science podcast. The photo looks as shown in the following screenshot:

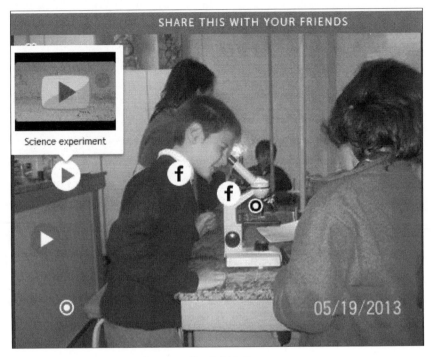

Image credit – Patricia Zamorano

Embedding images from thinglink.com

We have created an image using thinglink.com in the previous recipe. It is time to upload it in our Moodle course. This type of image is well suited for the summary section, so we will embed it there.

Getting ready

In order to embed the enhanced image that we have just created, we need to think of how to do it. We can use the URL, the HTML code, or any of the social networks available. We can share it using social networks if we have enabled a widget in our Moodle course. Let's see how to do it.

How to do it...

Now, go to http://www.thinglink.com/ and enter to our stream. We look for the image that we want to embed in our Moodle course; the one that we have just created. Follow these steps in order to get the code:

1. Click on **GO TO YOUR STREAM**.
2. Click on the photo to embed in our Moodle course.
3. Click on **Share**, as shown in the following screenshot:

4. Click on **COPY CODE TO CLIPBOARD**.
5. It is time to embed the photo in the Moodle course.

How it works...

We have just copied the code to embed in our Moodle course. We are to embed the photo in the **Summary** section because it will be the ice breaker for plenty of activities to work with. Choose the weekly outline section where we would edit the **Summary** section and follow these steps:

1. Click on the **Edit summary** icon.
2. Click on the **Edit HTML source** icon.

3. Paste the HTML code copied at `thinglink.com`.

4. Click on **Update**.

5. Click on **Save changes**.

6. When hovering the mouse over the image, there appears the links; for example, the screenshot shows the Facebook photos uploaded when clicking on the said link:

8
Working with Vector Graphics

In this chapter, we will cover the following recipes:

- ▸ Converting vector graphics to bitmap images
- ▸ Converting bitmaps to vector graphics
- ▸ Rendering parts of a converted vector drawing
- ▸ Embedding scalable vector graphics
- ▸ Improving vector graphics rendering with anti-aliasing
- ▸ Including vector graphics in OpenOffice documents
- ▸ Including vector graphics in PDF files
- ▸ Enhancing scalable vector graphics with hyperlinks

Introduction

This chapter explains how to work with different types of vector graphics formats. The recipes use diverse, free, and open source tools to edit, enhance, and convert different vector graphics files, covering the most common scenarios for multimedia Moodle activities. Vector graphics are one of the most difficult formats to handle in Moodle courses.

Inkscape is a free and open source vector-drawing software to be used in order to perform many recipes. It will allow us to work with many vector assets in several file formats and export them to a format recognized by Moodle. There are also online editing tools, which can be used to edit **SVG** (**Scalable Vector Graphics**) as well.

The recipes are organized in such a way, that they are linked among themselves. So, it would be a good idea to read the whole chapter in its order without skipping recipes because they add more information, as long as we advance on the recipes. We also use what we have created in the first recipes, to design the latest ones.

It is also very important to read the previous chapter, *Chapter 7, Working with Bitmaps and Photographs*. There are some aspects considered in that chapter that we are going to cover in this one.

Different types of vector graphics are involved in this chapter, due to the fact that they can enhance and create interactive activities. We can not only use them, but also modify them. It is like when we read something and we like to share a part of it with our students. So, we can also change the vector graphics in order to use a part of them.

Not only inserting the SVG graphics in Moodle is covered in this chapter, but also using them in other types of software, which can be uploaded to our Moodle courses. We are working in this chapter mainly with Inkscape, OpenOffice, and Adobe Reader; therefore, it would be a good idea for you to have them installed beforehand.

We can either design the SVG or look for one on the Internet; we will learn how to do it. We can modify the SVG and save it as another file extension. We may not need to use it as such, but just a part of it. We may insert the SVG in Moodle, or in other types of software, such as OpenOffice or PDF, using Adobe Reader.

We will use the same SVG in different recipes, to avoid looking for another graphic. We can save time and go over what we have just learned, instead of redesigning the activities again.

We are focusing on 2D and 3D geometry, though the information can be applied to any subject to be taught due to the fact that SVG files are needed to enhance our Moodle courses no matter what we are teaching. Images are a great asset to take into account when teaching because students do not read a plain and dull text. They look more appealing when an image is on it though.

Converting vector graphics to bitmap images

In this recipe, vector graphics are to be converted into bitmaps. That is to say, we do need to convert them because there is a process that we can carry out. It is very simple but we need to use free and open source software. Let's get ready!

Getting ready

This transformation process has to be done with the help of software such as Inkscape. Therefore, if you do not happen to have Inscape installed, you can download it from the following website: `http://inkscape.org/download/?lang=eng`.

Another option is to use free online editing software such as ImageBot. You can use it directly from your web browser at: `http://flamingtext.com/imagebot/editor`. So, now that we have the options, let's see how to do it.

How to do it...

It is time to find a place where we can search for vector graphics. There is a very interesting website, where we can find many kinds of icons: `http://www.openclipart.org/browse`. We can convert the SVG clipart using ImageBot. Therefore, we are going to follow these steps to start the transformation process:

1. Open your default web browser and enter `http://www.openclipart.org/browse`.

2. On the top-right margin, write `castle` in the search block.

3. Click on **Search**.

4. There appears many cliparts. Choose from one of them.

5. The clipart appears bigger, as shown in the following screenshot:

6. Click on the **Edit Image** button.

7. The SVG appears in the editing software, as shown in the following screenshot:

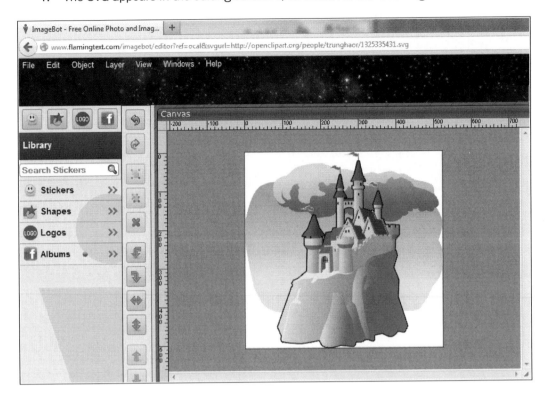

8. Select **File | Save**.

9. Save the file as `castle.svg`, for example.

10. Click on **Save** again.

11. There appears a pop-up window. Click on the **Save File** radio button and then click on **OK**.

How it works...

We are still working with the image editor. We have just selected the clipart and saved it as `.svg`. Now, it is time to transform this `.svg` into a bitmap (`.png` file). Therefore, these are the steps that we have to follow in order to carry out the transformation:

1. Click on **File | Save**.

2. Click on the down arrow next to **File Format** and choose **PNG**, as shown in the following screenshot:

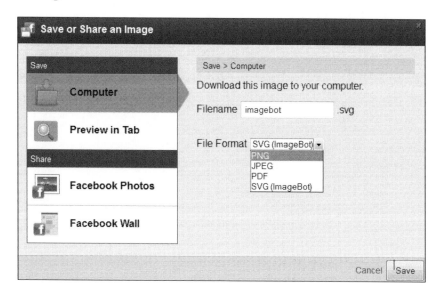

3. Click on **Save**.

4. There appears a pop-up window. Click on the **Save File** radio button and then click on **OK**.

5. We have transformed the drawing into a PNG format.

> PNG is an open format, which has lossless compression, as we have already dealt with in *Chapter 7, Working with Bitmaps and Photographs*. Moodle, Hot Potatoes, and Quandary 2 work very well with these types of files. We have worked with a PNG format due to the fact that the images are small in size.

Converting bitmaps to vector graphics

In this recipe, we go the other way round to the previous recipe. We convert a bitmap image such as a .png, .jpeg, or .gif into a .svg. We work with an online tool to vectorize the bitmap using http://vectormagic.com/home. The steps to follow are very simple and there are plenty of features to take into account when vectorizing.

We can load the bitmap image from the clipboard or by uploading the file from our computer. Once the image is uploaded into the application we can start working. We can work with the previous image of the castle. So, let's get ready.

Getting ready

We convert bitmap images, which are made up by pixels into vector images, which in turn are made up by shapes. The shapes are mathematical descriptions of images and when selected they do not become pixelated when scaling up. Vector graphics can handle scaling without problems.

Vector images are the preferred type to work with in graphic design on paper or clothes, the opposed of a bitmap image, which looks great on the screen. Furthermore, vector graphics are used for flash animations in the web.

How to do it...

We need to open our default web browser and go to the following website: `http://vectormagic.com/home`. There are two options to work with the editor, either online or download the desktop version. We are to work online, so these are the steps that we have to follow:

1. Click on **Upload Image To Trace ....**

2. Browse for the bitmap image to upload and click on **Open**, as shown in the following screenshot:

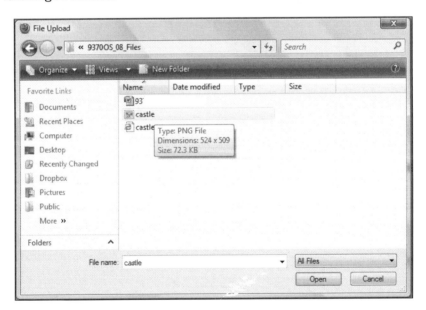

3. When scaling up, the PNG format looks more blurred than the SVG format. The images can be compared, as shown in the following screenshot:

How it works...

We have just converted our bitmap into a .svg format. Using the editor we can customize the color, edit the results, or remove the background. There are plenty of options to work with, but that is not the aim of the recipe.

After editing the image and getting the desired result, we can save the .svg in our computer, so follow these steps:

1. Click on **Download Result**.
2. Write your e-mail address in the **Email** block.
3. Click on **I accept. Create my account**.
4. You will receive an e-mail with a link to download the image. Click on it.
5. Click on **Enable download**, as shown in the following screenshot:

6. Click on **SVG**, as shown in the following screenshot:

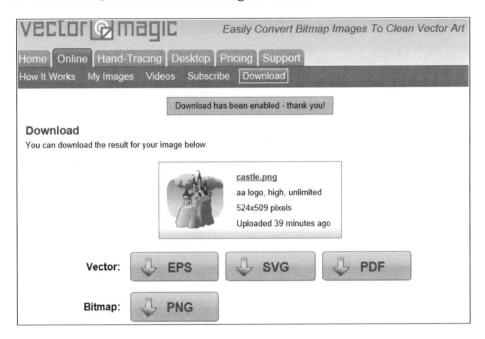

7. Click on **Save File**, and save the file on your computer.

Rendering parts of a converted vector drawing

In this recipe, we will work with Inkscape. We have previously mentioned this software in the first recipe; we can download it from the following website: `http://inkscape.org/download/?lang=eng`. We have converted a `.png` into a `.svg` in the previous recipe, and we can add more SVG using the drawing options in Inkscape. After creating the graphic we will render some of its parts.

Getting ready

First of all, let's click on the Inkscape icon on our desktop, (or run the Inkscape software) because we need to use this software. In the previous recipe, we have worked with a castle image, so let's add stars to the castle, because we can combine shapes and create an activity sharing both of them. We can also remove the flags of the castle. So, imagine that we have a file but we want to use only a part of it. It looks as if you have an article in a magazine and you need to take out the advertisement.

How to do it...

When we think of rendering parts of vector graphics, we mean that we are going to use a part of a drawing that we have designed. Therefore, we will not use all the shapes in the file; we will save some of them, which we are to select before exporting them. This is the aim of this recipe. That is to say, to transform the selection in a bitmap.

Run the Inkscape software, and follow these steps:

1. Click on **File | Open...**. Now, look for the file to open (castle) and click on **Open**.

2. Click on the **Select and transform objects** icon and select the flag of the castle, as shown in the following screenshot:

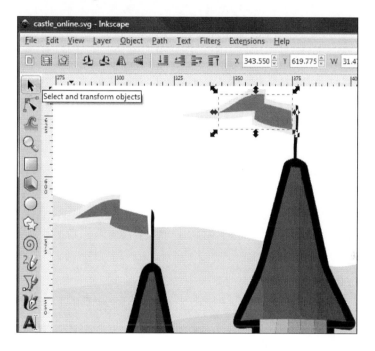

3. Press the *Delete* key.

4. Repeat steps 2 and 3 to remove the remaining flags.

5. Click on **Create stars and polygons (*)** on the left-hand side margin, as shown in the following screenshot:

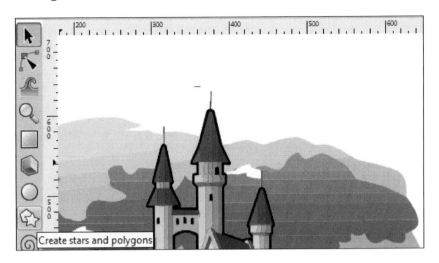

6. Draw several stars of different sizes around the castle.

7. Right-click on one of the stars. A pop-up context menu appears and choose **Fill and Stroke**, as shown in the following screenshot:

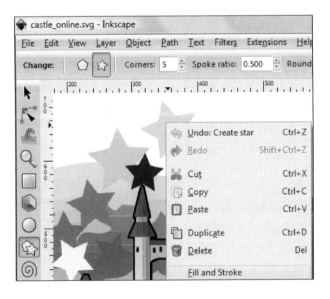

8. Another window on the right-hand margin appears and you can change the color or you can add stripes to the shapes, as you click on each of them.

9. When you finish, click on the **Select and transform objects** icon.

10. Draw a rectangle over the area that you need to use. Start outside the drawing.

11. The selected area appears, as shown in the following screenshot:

12. To save the file, click on **File | Save as ...** and write a name for the file.

How it works...

We have just rendered parts of the drawing of a castle and added some stars. We have used some of them. It was a simple drawing but we can also do the same process with others that we just want to use a part of them. We can export the drawing as a bitmap. These are the steps that we have to follow:

1. Click on **File | Export Bitmap...**.

2. A pop-up window appears; on its ribbon **Selection** is highlighted.

3. Export the parts of the drawing, selected on the left, as shown in the previous screenshot.

4. Click on **Browse...**, write a name, and save the file.

5. Click on **Export**, as shown in the following screenshot:

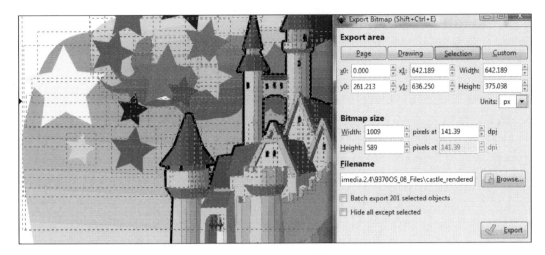

6. The file looks as shown in the following screenshot:

Embedding scalable vector graphics

It is a very interesting recipe to perform and to work with. There are different ways of uploading files in our Moodle courses. The steps that we have to follow have to be together, that is to say, it is not advisable to do them separately or edit the activity because they might not work.

Getting ready

We are dealing with a pure SVG and it is advisable that we use Mozilla Firefox web browser or Internet Explorer 9 because it might not work with other web browsers. So, let's see how to do this recipe!

How to do it...

We have already used the castle and stars images in the previous recipes, so we can change the shape or keep working with them. We can create other drawings using Inkscape. Once we have designed the drawings, enter the Moodle course and choose the weekly outline section where we want to add the activity and follow these steps:

1. Click on **Add an activity or resource**.
2. Click on **Assignment | Add**.
3. Complete the **Assignment name** block.
4. Complete the **Description** block.
5. Highlight a word or phrase and click on the **Insert/edit link** icon, as shown in the following screenshot:

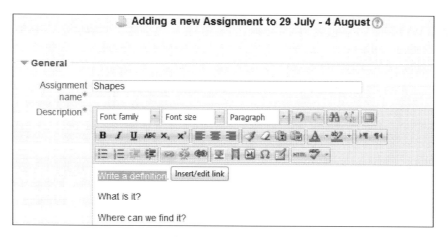

6. Click on **Browse** next to the **Link URL** block, as shown in the following screenshot:

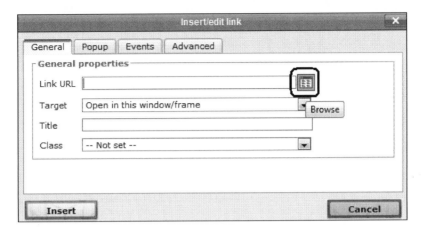

7. Click on **Upload a file | Browse...** and look for the file that we have just created.

8. Select the file and then click on **Open | Upload this file**.

9. Click on **Insert**. The image will not appear, because we need to work with code.

How it works...

We have just designed and started to insert the SVG in our Moodle course. Therefore, we need to embed it. In this recipe, we need to work with some code! Thus, these are the steps that you are going to follow to see the SVG in the course:

1. Click on **Edit HTML Source**. Some code will appear. We are going to edit the code. The following code will appear on the HTML source editor. The only difference will be the location of the file (`http://localhost/draftfile.php/5/user/draft/170166016/castle.svg`):

```
<p><a href=
"http://localhost/draftfile.php/5/user/draft/170166016
/castle.svg">Write a definition</a>.</p>
<p>What is it?</p>
<p>Where can we find it?</p>
```

2. We have to add the following code in order to embed the spiral, or any SVG file that you want to upload on our Moodle course:

```
<object type="image/svg+xml" data="
http://localhost/draftfile.php/5/user/draft/170166016/
castle.svg">
</object>
</p>
```

3. You must bear in mind that the name of the file previously linked is the same in the code that we insert. Otherwise it won't work!

4. Click on **Update**.

5. Check the **Online text** checkbox.

6. Click on **Save and display** to check and see how it works, as shown in the following screenshot:

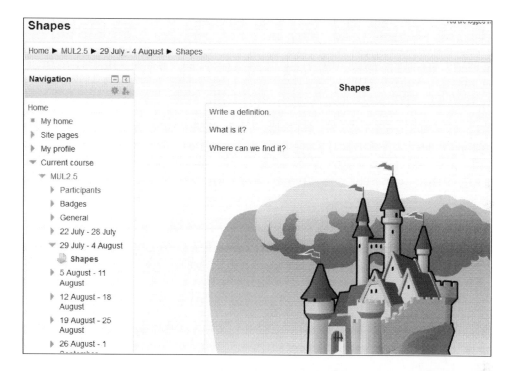

Improving vector graphics rendering with anti-aliasing

In this recipe, we continue using the castle image. Therefore, it means that we also need Inkscape. The aim of this recipe is to export the whole graphic with a low resolution. Anti-aliasing is displayed in medium resolution and it can be shown as a blur image. We are always looking for clear and smooth lines in our graphics.

Anti-aliasing is the technique used in order to minimize the distortion artifacts.

Getting ready

We need to work with Inkscape, as mentioned previously. We can open the file that we have created in the previous recipe or we can create a new drawing.

Anti-aliasing applies intermediate colors in order to eliminate pixels, that is to say the saw tooth of pixelated lines. Therefore, we need to look for a lower resolution so that the saw tooth effect does not appear when we make the graphic bigger.

How to do it...

As was mentioned, we need to start the Inkscape software in order to work with an SVG. Therefore, these steps have to be followed to render the image with anti-aliasing:

1. Click on **File | Open**.

2. Open `castle.svg` or another file with the same extension, as shown in the following screenshot:

3. Click on **File | Export Bitmap...**.

4. Click on **Browse...**, write a name, and save the file.

5. Click on **Export**.

How it works...

If we follow the previous steps mentioned, we get the SVG with the anti-aliasing effect, which Inkscape already has. Therefore, the image will look smoother and cleaner than the previous one. The following screenshot shows two images. The image on the left is the one to which we applied anti-aliasing and the one on the right is the one without anti-aliasing:

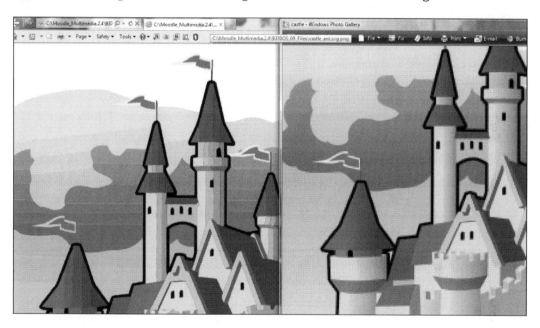

Including vector graphics in OpenOffice documents

We design this recipe using OpenOffice. We can download it from the following website: http://www.openoffice.org/download/. We are going to work with OpenOffice presentation. Another option is to use Microsoft Office PowerPoint. If you happen to work with this software, the steps are similar.

Getting ready

It is time to look for an SVG graphic to insert in our presentation. As our baseline topic in this chapter is 2D and 3D geometry, our SVG is to be with shapes. We can insert the castle with stars designed in the previous recipe. In that case, we can combine the activities in our Moodle course. We can insert the graphic in the weekly outline section to introduce the topic, and we can now use the SVG graphic to design an activity. We can also render the drawing as we did in the previous recipes, in case we do not want to use the whole of it.

How to do it...

We have already used OpenOffice in the previous recipes so we have already installed it on our system, which may appear on the desktop of the computer. To start, click on its icon and run this software. These are the steps that you have to follow:

1. Click on **Presentation**.

2. A pop-up window with the name **Presentation Wizard** appears. Click on **Next**.

3. Under the **Select a slide design** heading, choose **Water**, to surround the castle that will be inserted.

4. Click on **Next**.

5. Under the **Select a slide transition** heading, choose the **Shape Diamond** effect to keep the shapes idea.

6. Click on **Create**, as shown in the following screenshot:

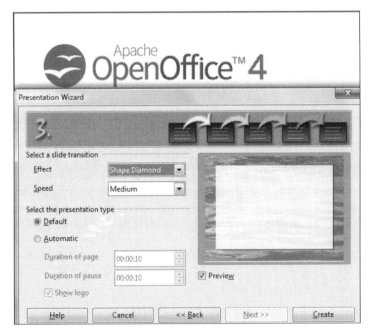

7. On the right-hand margin, there appears a **Layouts** pane that you may choose in order to design the presentation. Choose one with the name **Title and 2 Content**. When hovering the mouse on it, it says what you can insert, as shown in the following screenshot:

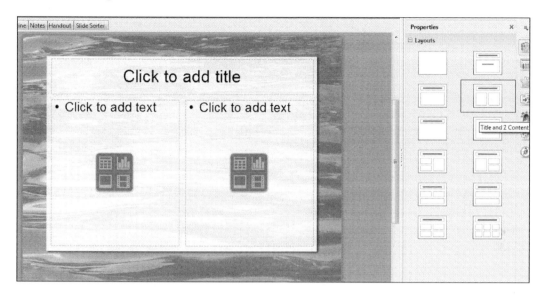

8. Double-click on the chosen layout.

9. Click on **Click to add title** and write the title.

10. Click on **Insert Picture**, as shown in the following screenshot:

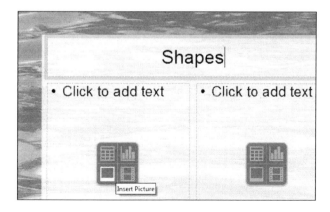

11. Look for the image (SVG) to upload, select the image, and click on **Open**.

12. Click on **Click to add text** and write a comment on the castle.

13. You can click on **Insert | Slide** and add more content to the presentation.

14. To save the file, click on **File | Save as ...** and write a name for the file. Now click on **Save**.

How it works...

After designing the presentation and saving it, we can upload it to our Moodle course. It is the introduction to an activity. Therefore, we can add a resource to our course. So, choose the weekly outline section where you want to add the resource and follow these steps:

1. Click on **Add an activity or resource**.

2. Click on **File | Add**.

3. Complete the **Name** and **Description** blocks.

4. Click on **Add...** within the **Content** block.

5. Click on **Upload a file | Browse...** and look for the file to be uploaded.

6. Click on **Open | Upload this file**.

7. Within **Appearance**, click on the down arrow next to **Display** and choose **Embed**.

8. Click on **Save and display**.

9. When students click on the activity, it looks as shown in the following screenshot:

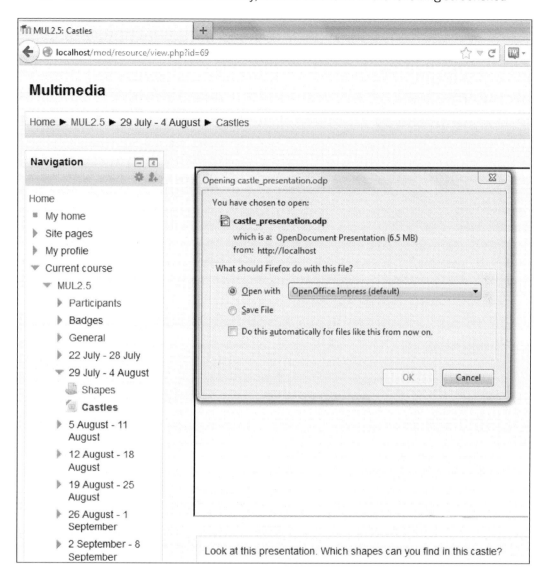

Including vector graphics in PDF files

This is a very simple recipe. We have designed in the previous recipe a file in OpenOffice in which we included an SVG. So, we can use the same file to work with, in order to avoid some steps. Let's get ready!

Getting ready

What we need to have installed is OpenOffice, which we have already used in the previous recipes, and Adobe Reader. We can download the last software from: `http://get.adobe.com/reader/`.

How to do it...

We open the file in OpenOffice and we only make a little change to it, in order to export it as PDF. It is very simple. We are just a click away, we can say. First of all, start OpenOffice presentation and open the file that we have just created in the previous recipe. Then, follow these steps:

1. Click on **File | Export as PDF...**, as shown in the following screenshot:

2. Click on **Export**.
3. Write a name for the file and click on **Save**.

How it works...

We have just saved the file as PDF. It is time to open the file in Adobe Reader. There are SVGs, therefore, we have included them in PDF files. You can also perform the same procedure using Microsoft Office or any other type of OpenOffice options. In this case, we converted a presentation into a PDF, but we can convert a text file as well. The file looks as shown in the following screenshot:

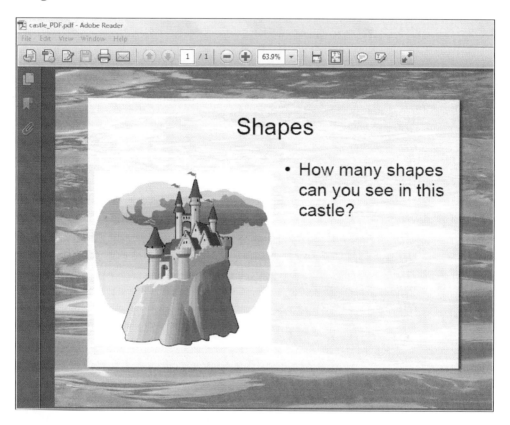

We can upload this file to our Moodle course in the same way that we did in the previous recipe.

Enhancing scalable vector graphics with hyperlinks

In this recipe, we need to use Inkscape again. We have become quite familiar with the software, as we have used it many times. This time we will create hyperlinks on the SVG graphics. When students click on the image, they will open a website.

Getting ready

We can continue working with the image of the castle. We can add links to the different parts of the castle and find its definitions in the web. So, when clicking on the parts of the castle, a website is displayed related to the definition of that part and there appears some information as well.

How to do it...

We need to start the Inkscape software in order to design the hyperlinks. We open the file that we have been working with `castle.svg`. Therefore, let's run Inkscape and follow these steps:

1. Click on a part of the castle.

2. Right-click on the said part. There appears a pop-up menu. Choose **Create Link**, as shown in the following screenshot:

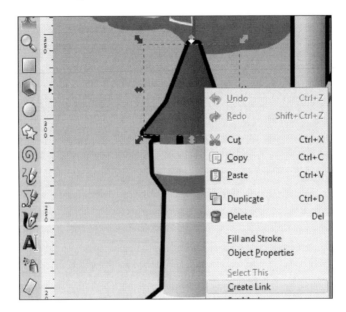

3. Right-click again on the same shape and then click on **Link Properties**.

4. A pop-up window appears. Complete the **Href** block with the website that you want to make the link that is to give additional information about the SVG, as shown in the following screenshot:

5. Close the pop-up window.

6. Save the file. Click on **File | Save as...**, write a name, and save the file.

How it works...

We have just enhanced SVG with hyperlinks using the Inkscape software; therefore, it is time to see how it works. We can upload the graphic to our Moodle course as we have already done it before using code.

Another option is to open the file in your web browser. Remember that it is advisable to open SVG files in Mozilla Firefox or in Internet Explorer 9 where these files work properly. When you click on the graphic, another window opens showing the website of the hyperlink. It is shown in the following screenshot:

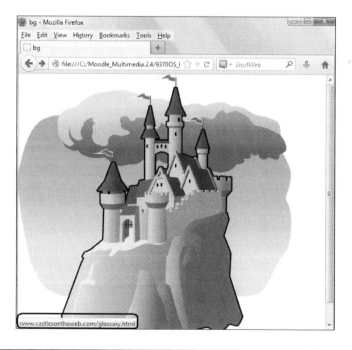

When hovering the mouse over the part where we have inserted the link, we can see the link in the screenshot at the bottom of the browser; in this case using the Mozilla Firefox web browser. When we click on it, the website is displayed.

9
Designing and Integrating Repositories and E-portfolios

In this chapter, we will cover the following recipes:

- ▶ Enabling the Box.net repository
- ▶ Working with Box.net
- ▶ Enabling the Flickr repository
- ▶ Working with Flickr
- ▶ Enabling portfolios
- ▶ Enabling the File Download portfolio
- ▶ Working with the Alfresco repository
- ▶ Enabling the Alfresco repository

Introduction

This chapter explains how to design and integrate repositories and e-portfolios into Moodle courses. We will also learn interesting techniques to organize the information for our students as well as combine everything learned so far. Besides this, finding information in online repositories is also shown in this chapter.

The recipes are short and precise; therefore, the most important aspects are to be covered in this chapter. We will take a look at some of the most relevant repositories and portfolios available until now in Moodle.

An interesting repository that is worth paying attention to is Box.net. We need to sign up for an account, in order to create an application and get the Box.net API (short for Application Programming Interface) key so as to enable it in our Moodle course.

In order to gain benefits out of repositories in Moodle, they must be enabled. Therefore, the recipes in this chapter, as in the previous ones, have been designed in a way that it is best to read them in order because they are interrelated.

An **e-portfolio** (electronic portfolio or digital portfolio) is a collection of electronic evidence gathered and administered by a user on the Web. The evidence should be inputted files, images, and text, among other types of files. Furthermore, e-portfolios in Moodle 2.x enable information to be exported to external systems.

It is very interesting to enable both repositories and portfolios, because we learn how to use them. Besides, another characteristic to be considered as an advantage is that portfolios gather files saved on the web, not on our computer. That is to say, that we can change the files anywhere. We do not need to have our computer, just an Internet connection so we can just log in and edit the files we need!

To sum up, we could say that repositories and e-portfolios are easy to back up, have a good portability as well as shelf life. Therefore, it would be advisable that we consider them, when we design any Moodle course, to use them and teach our students to use them too.

It is also important to mention that the administrator of the Moodle course must enable both repositories and e-portfolios; otherwise, we will not be able to use them. Without having an administrator's consent, the teacher cannot use any of these.

Enabling the Box.net repository

The first recipe of this chapter starts by showing how to enable the Box.net repository in our Moodle course. The Moodle administrator has to enable it; otherwise, we cannot have access to its benefits. Box.net "offers secure, scalable content sharing" as it is described on the website. So, before enabling the repository, we have to sign up.

Getting ready

We need to create an account in Box.net before enabling the repository. So, we go to the website `https://app.box.com/pricing/` and sign up. After doing so, it is also advisable to upload some content as well, so that after enabling it we can work with it in order to verify that it works.

How to do it...

Enabling a repository takes a few steps. We need to follow a process in order to do it. The first repository to enable is Box.net, so these are the steps to follow (in your Moodle):

1. Click on **Site administration**.
2. Click on **Plugins**, as shown in the following screenshot:

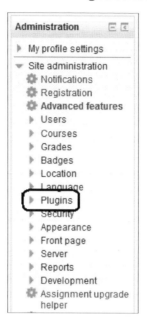

3. Click on **Repositories | Manage repositories**.
4. Click on the drop-down menu next to **Box.net** and choose **Enabled and visible**, as shown in the following screenshot:

5. Minimize the Moodle course window.

6. Launch your default web browser and enter `https://www.box.com/`.

7. Log in to your Box.net account or sign in with your Google account.

How it works...

We have just enabled the option of the Box.net repository, so that it is visible inside the plugins list. To finish the enabling process, we need to get the API key. (API stands for Application Programming Interface.) Moodle incorporates a third-party API so that repository developers can develop more efficient plugins in order to integrate the repository in Moodle.

Maximize the Moodle course window. In order to enable Box.net, we need to paste its API key in our Moodle course window. After following the steps hereinbefore mentioned, we are taken to a new page. Then, follow these steps:

1. Right-click on **Box.net developer page**.

2. There appears a pop-up window. Click on **Open Link in New Window**, as shown in the following screenshot:

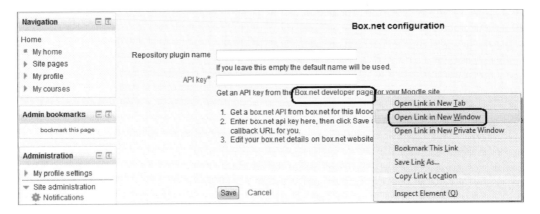

3. Click on **Create New Application**.

4. Complete the **Application name** block.

5. Click on **Content API**, as shown in the following screenshot:

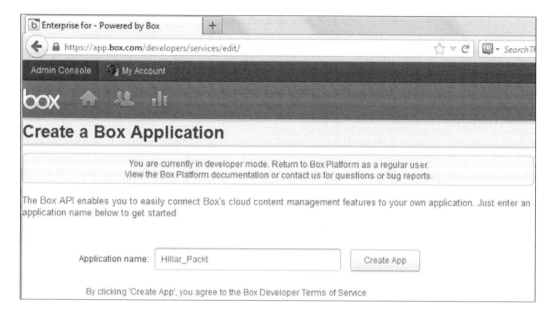

6. Highlight the API key and copy it, as shown in the following screenshot:

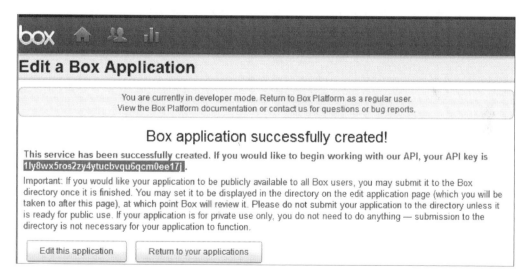

7. Minimize the Box.net window.

8. Maximize the Moodle administration window.

9. Write a name inside the **Repository plugin name** block, the same as in **Application name**.

10. Paste the API key.

11. Click on **Save**.

See also

▶   The *Working with Box.net* recipe

Working with Box.net

In the previous recipe, we have started enabling Box.net. We are just a click away from finishing. Therefore, in this recipe we will work with Box.net as well, so that we can share the content that we have uploaded in our Box.net account, as it was suggested in the previous recipe when creating an account.

Getting ready

We need to enter our Moodle course and get the callback URL in order to paste it in our Box. net account. We need to link both of the software in order to be connected. In the other part of the recipe we work with Box.net as a repository, so that we can check if it is enabled and we can share content with it.

How to do it...

We need to follow the last step in order to finish enabling the Box.net repository. We need to keep working with both windows of Box.net and our Moodle course. We maximize our Moodle site, and when we go back to it after saving the changes, we click on **Settings** next to **Box.net** and follow these steps:

1. Highlight the redirect URL.

2. Right-click on it. There appears a pop-up window. Click on **Copy**, as shown in the following screenshot:

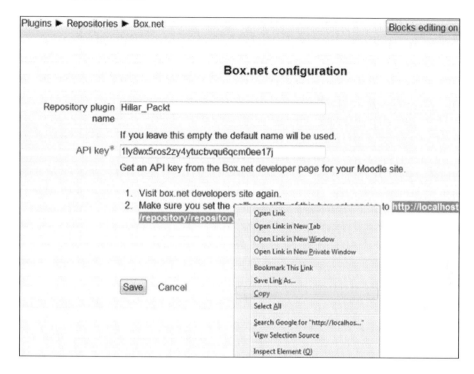

3. Click on **Save**.

4. Minimize the Moodle course window.

5. Maximize the Box.net window.

6. Click on **Edit this Application**.

7. Paste the redirect URL within the **Redirect url** block, as shown in the following screenshot:

8. Click on **Save service**.

How it works...

Box.net is finally enabled. We can add a resource in order to use our enabled repository. We choose the weekly outline section where we want to add the resource, and follow these steps:

1. Click on **Add an activity or resource**.

2. Select **File** and then click on **Add**.

3. Complete the **Name** and **Description** blocks.

4. Click on **Add...** within the **Content** block.

5. Click on the icon with the repository plugin name that you created, on the left hand side.

6. You may need to log in, in order to use Box.net. If so, a pop-up window appears and then the files and folders appear in the file picker, as shown in the following screenshot:

7. Click on the file to be uploaded. A pop-up window appears.

8. Click on **Select this file**.

9. Click on **Save and display**.

Enabling the Flickr repository

We have already used Flickr in the previous chapters so we must have an account; otherwise, it is advisable to have one in order to work with the repository. We can enable two Flickr repositories. We are to deal with one, though.

Getting ready

We need to have a Flickr account with some content to work with after the repository is enabled so we can add images, which can be used in the Moodle course in order to create a resource or an activity afterwards.

The advantage of dealing with a repository is that we do not need to carry our laptop anywhere. We can design the course using all the content that we want, which is stored in these places.

How to do it...

We need to follow some similar steps as the ones we did in the first recipe of this chapter. So, we know that it is simple once we enable the first repository. These are the steps that we have to follow:

1. Click on **Site administration** | **Plugins** | **Repositories** | **Manage repositories**.
2. Click on the drop-down menu next to **Flickr** and choose **Enabled and visible**, as shown in the following screenshot:

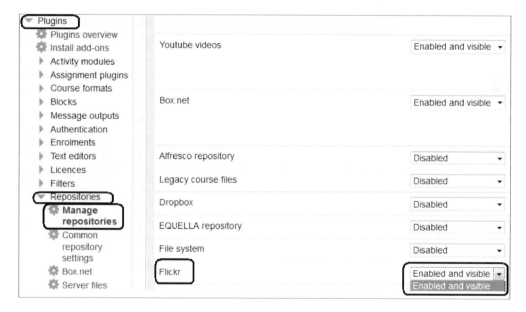

3. Minimize the Moodle site.
4. Launch your default web browser and enter `http://www.flickr.com/`.
5. Log in to your Flickr account or sign in with your Google or Facebook account.

How it works...

We have just enabled the option of the Flickr repository, so that it is visible inside the plugins list. To proceed to the enabling process, we need to get the API key. Maximize the Moodle course window and paste the API key in it. After following the steps hereinbefore mentioned, we are taken to a new page. Then, follow these steps:

1. Right-click on **Flickr API Key and Secret**.

2. There appears a pop-up menu. Click on **Open Link in New Window**, as shown in the following screenshot:

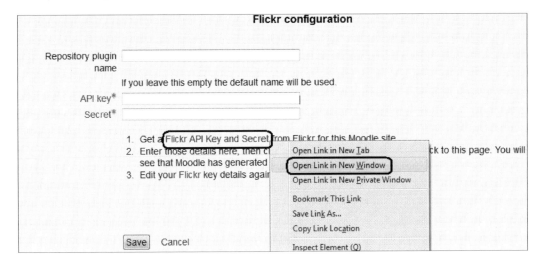

3. Click on **Get Another Key**, as shown in the following screenshot:

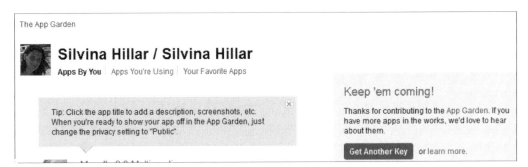

4. Click on **APPLY FOR A NON-COMMERCIAL KEY** (if its content suits your needs, otherwise choose a commercial key).

5. Complete the necessary blocks, as shown in the following screenshot:

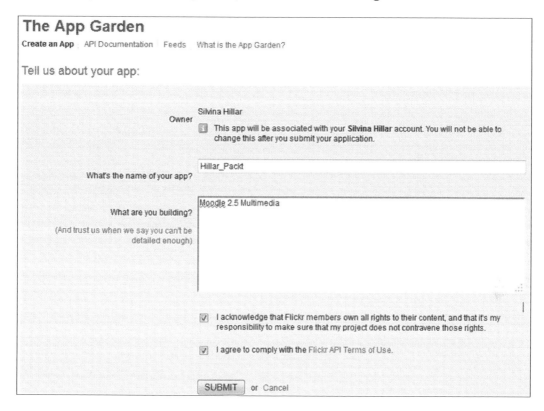

6. Click on **SUBMIT**.

7. Highlight the **Key** and copy it. Minimize Flickr.

8. Maximize the Moodle course window and paste it in the **API key** field. Minimize it.

9. Maximize Flickr and highlight the **Secret** and copy it, as shown in the following screenshot:

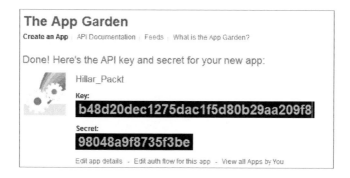

> It is important to bear in mind that the key and the secret must not be shared. In this case it is only shown without having any relevant information more than a screenshot of a cookbook, but these are like passwords, very secret.

10. Minimize Flickr.

11. Maximize the Moodle course window and paste it in the **Secret** field.

12. Complete the **Repository plugin name** block, the same as **What's the name of your app?** block in Flickr. It can be seen in the following screenshot:

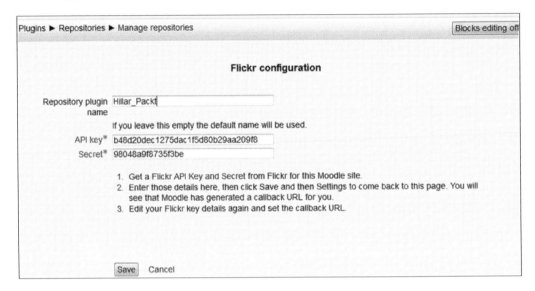

13. Click on **Save**.

See also

▶ The *Working with Flickr* recipe

Working with Flickr

We are just a few clicks away to finishing enabling the Flickr repository. So, we have to work with both windows at the same time to copy and paste the necessary information. The process is similar as the one with Box.net.

Getting ready

We can upload more content to work with our repository, because in this recipe we integrate it in our Moodle course. We can create either a resource or an activity in order to use it.

How to do it...

We need to finish the Flickr configuration process. So, after saving the changes in our Moodle course, we click on **Settings** next to **Flickr**. These are the steps that we have to follow:

1. Highlight the callback URL and right-click on it.

2. A pop-up window appears. Click on **Copy**, as shown in the following screenshot:

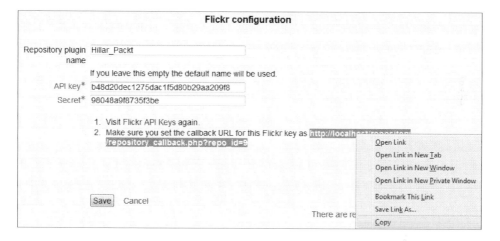

3. Click on **Save**.

4. Minimize the Moodle course window.

5. Maximize Flickr.

6. Scroll down the page and click on **App Garden**, as shown in the following screenshot:

About Flickr	Community	Help	Apps and the API
Who we are	Community Guidelines	Need help? Start here!	Flickr for mobile
Flickr blog	Report abuse	Help forum	App Garden
Jobs		FAQs	API documentation
			Developer blog
			Developer Guide

7. Click on **Apps By You**, on the right-hand margin.

8. Click on the App that you have just created.

9. Click on **Edit**, on the right-hand margin, as shown in the following screenshot:

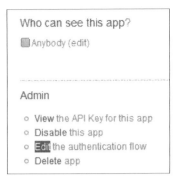

10. Paste the link in the **Callback URL** block, as shown in the following screenshot:

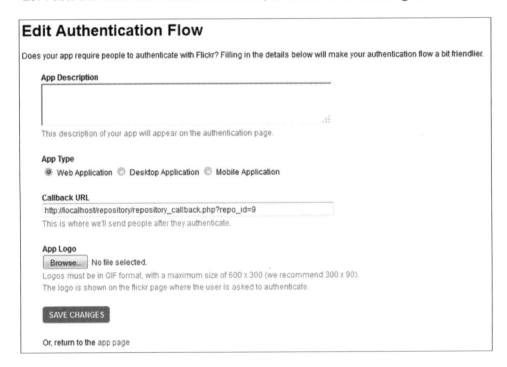

11. Click on **SAVE CHANGES**.

How it works...

We can design an activity or resource using our Flickr account. The repository that we created can store images, which can be used in our Moodle course. We can store whatever we need in order to design our courses.

Enter your Moodle course and choose the weekly outline section where we want to insert the resource. These are the steps that we have to follow:

1. Click on **Add an activity or resource**.

2. Select **Page** and then click on **Add**.

3. Complete the **Name** and **Description** blocks.

4. Within the **Content** block, click on the **Insert/edit image** icon (sixth icon in the last row).

5. Click on **Find or upload an image....**

6. Click on the Flickr appname that you created and then click on **Login**.

7. Click on **OK, I'LL AUTHORIZE IT**, as shown in the following screenshot:

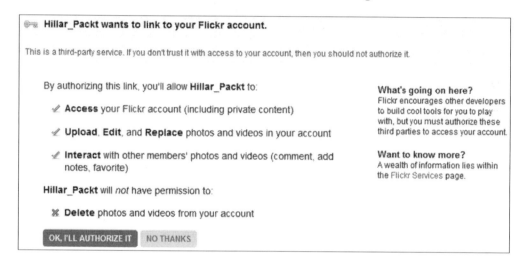

8. Click on **Upload a file** and select a file from your system to upload.

9. Click on **Upload this file**.

10. Click on **Insert**.

11. Click on **Save and return to course**.

Enabling portfolios

In this recipe we start enabling portfolios, showing how to enable a portfolio in our Moodle course. If we do not enable it, we cannot have access to its benefits. One of the advantages is that content from our Moodle course can be exported to a virtual and stable external portfolio. So, let's get ready!

Getting ready

The Moodle.org website reads "Enabling the use of portfolios in Moodle is a 2-step process for a site administrator". Thus, we must have access to the administration of the site or ask the Moodle site administrator to do so.

How to do it...

First of all, we need to follow the main step, so that the portfolio is enabled under **Site administration**. That is to say, that we have to enable it in order to see that we can enable the different portfolios. If we do not take that step, we would never be able to see it or use it.

So, if we do not have access to the administration of the course, ask the administrator to take these steps:

1. Click on **Site administration | Advanced features**.

2. Click on **Enable portfolios**, as shown in the following screenshot:

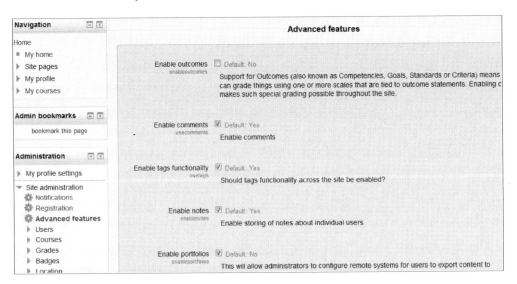

3. Click on **Save changes**.

How it works...

We have just successfully enabled the feature to enable portfolios on our Moodle site. It is a very simple recipe, but a very important step to bear in mind before working with portfolios on our Moodle site. Otherwise, we will not be able to enable any of them. We can see that the portfolios are ready to be configured because they appear under **Plugins**, as shown in the following screenshot:

Enabling the File Download portfolio

We have just enabled the **Portfolios** option, so that it is visible inside the **Plugins** list. There are many portfolios, which can be enabled in Moodle. One of them is **File download** through which we can download the content from the Moodle activities.

Getting ready

We need to enter our Moodle course and look for an activity that we want to download in our files. We can choose a forum activity so that we can download the entire conversation of students. We need to know what to work with in order to use the portfolio.

How to do it...

File download is very simple to enable, that is the reason why we start with this portfolio. Therefore, let's take advantage of these few steps and follow them in order to start making portfolios visible in our Moodle course:

1. Click on **Site administration | Plugins | Portfolios | Manage portfolios**.
2. Click on the drop-down menu next to **File download** and choose **Enable and visible**, as shown in the following screenshot:

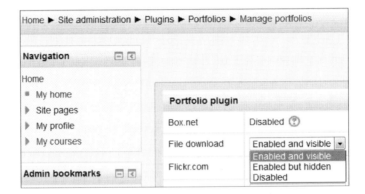

3. Click on **Save | Continue**.
4. Click on **Home**.

How it works...

Enter any Moodle course created. Search for the results or find a chat or forum activity that we have already created. In this recipe, we go to the course **Traveling around the World and Watching the Universe**. This course was created during a recipe in *Chapter 2, Working with 2D and 3D Maps*. We will focus on the result of the forum activity **Traveling to the Moon**. Therefore, these are the steps that we have to follow in order to save our course to a portfolio using **File Download**:

1. Enter the Moodle course.
2. Click on **Traveling to the Moon** forum activity (or any other forum activity that you want to export).

3. Click on the discussion topic that you want to save, in this case **Travelling to the Moon**, as shown in the following screenshot:

4. Click on the drop-down menu to select the way you want to see the forum answers, as shown in the following screenshot:

5. Click on **Export whole discussion**, on the left-hand side margin.

6. Click on **Next**.

7. Click on **Continue**.

8. The following message appears in our Moodle course and there appears a pop-up window asking either to **Open with** or **Save File**, as shown in the following screenshot:

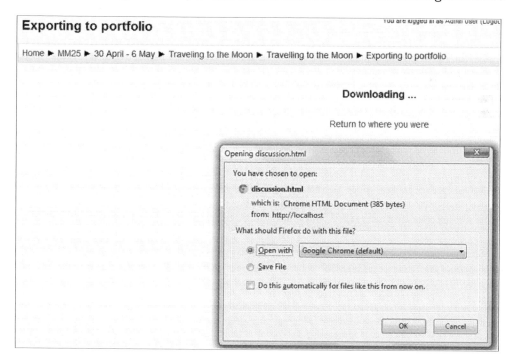

9. Click on an alternative and click **OK**.

10. You can choose to **Return to where you were**.

11. Click on **Home**.

Working with the Alfresco repository

In this recipe we work with the Alfresco repository. Although, it is enabled as a repository, we can use it as a portfolio as well. That is to say, we can store whatever we need in the cloud, and we can upload it to our Moodle course, without even having our device at hand. So, we are enabling a portfolio as a repository; it is similar to Box.net but the steps are different.

Getting ready

We need to create an account in Alfresco and upload some content in order to use it. So, we have to go to the website `http://www.alfresco.com/tour`, and create an account. We must bear in mind that we need to create an account using the work e-mail, due to the fact that free e-mail addresses are not accepted at the moment of writing. Since Alfresco accepts work e-mails, they also accept e-mails from schools, so we must have an account either from our work, or institution.

How to do it...

We need to create an account and upload some files in order to use them afterwards in our Moodle course. So, these are the necessary steps that we have to follow in order to start working with Alfresco:

1. Complete the e-mail block and click on **Get Started**, as shown in the following screenshot:

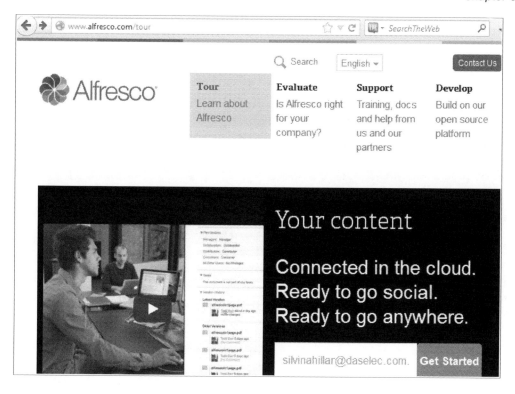

2. Minimize the Alfresco window.

3. Open your e-mail inbox. You must have received a non-reply message from Alfresco.

4. Click on **Activate account**, as shown in the following screenshot:

5. Complete the necessary blocks in order to complete the profile.

6. Click on **Continue**.

7. You will be taken to your dashboard.

8. Click on **Create Site**. (You need to create your portfolio within the Alfresco website in order to store files there.)

9. There appears a pop-up window.

10. Complete the necessary blocks, as shown in the following screenshot:

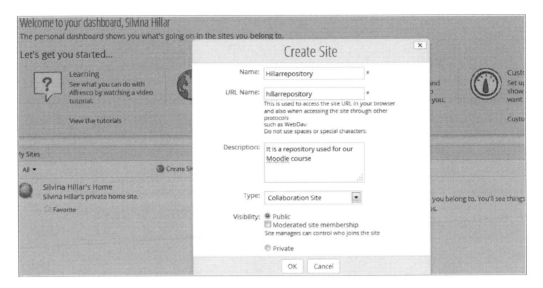

11. Click on **OK**.

How it works...

We have just created an account in our new repository. We need to add some content in it. We just add some files in order to use them afterwards in our Moodle course. Follow these steps:

1. Click on **Upload content**, as shown in the following screenshot:

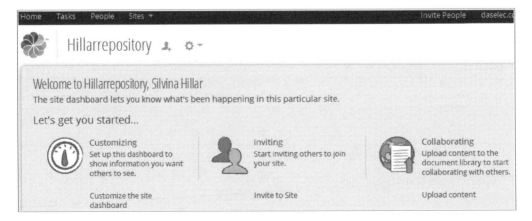

2. There appears a pop-up window.

3. Click on **Select files to upload**, select the file to be uploaded and then click on **Open**.

4. Repeat the previous step as many times as the number of files you need to upload.

There are plenty of features to be explored using Alfresco, which make it a wonderful portfolio in order to store content. We can also create content using the Google Docs document by clicking on the **Create Content...** button within the upper ribbon.

See also

▸ The *Enabling the Alfresco repository* recipe

Enabling the Alfresco repository

We have just uploaded some content to our "cloud portfolio" in the previous recipe. Now, it is time to enable it on our Moodle site, so that we can upload the said content to it. It takes some steps to do it; we need to work with two windows in order to enable it.

Getting ready

We have to enter our Moodle site in order to start enabling the Alfresco repository. There are some steps that we have to follow. The first steps are similar, but when Alfresco is enabled and visible, we need to get some information from the Alfresco website in order to enable it.

How to do it...

We need to enter our Moodle course. Now, these are the necessary steps that we have to follow in order to start enabling the Alfresco repository:

1. Click on **Site administration | Plugins | Repositories | Manage repositories**.

2. Click on the drop-down menu next to **Alfresco repository** and select **Enabled and visible**, as shown in the following screenshot:

3. Tick both checkboxes, as shown in the following screenshot:

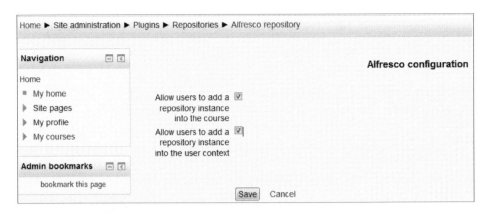

4. Click on **Save**.

5. Click on **Settings** of **Alfresco repository**.

6. Click on **Create a repository instance**.

7. Complete the **Name** block, writing the name used in Alfresco.

8. Copy the URL form from your Alfresco Dashboard and paste it in **Alfresco URL** in the Moodle course window, as shown in the following screenshot:

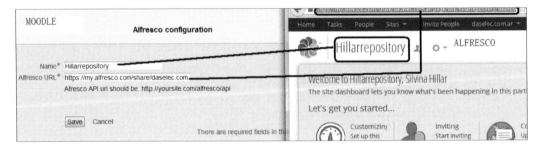

9. Click on **Save**.

10. Click on **Home**.

How it works...

We have just enabled the Alfresco repository. It is time to take advantage of it. So, we can add a resource in our Moodle course in order to use it. Choose the weekly outline section where we want to add the resource. These are the steps that you have to follow in order to do so:

1. Click on **Add an activity or resource**.
2. Select **File** and then click on **Add**.
3. Complete the **Name** and **Description** blocks.
4. In the **Content** block click on **Add...**. Within the **File picker** there appears your Alfresco repository, as shown in the following screenshot:

5. Complete the **User name** and **Password** blocks.
6. Click on **Submit**.
7. Click on the files to be uploaded.
8. Click on **Save and return to course**.

Index

Symbols

3D images
URL 213
3D maps
drawing, 3DVIA Shape for Maps used 61-66
3DVIA Shape for Maps
URL 61
used, for drawing 3D maps 61-66

A

Adobe files
working with HTML code, embedding 120, 121
Adobe Reader
URL 117
Alfresco
URL 268
Alfresco repository
enabling 271-273
working with 268-271
animated 3D graphics
creating 213-216
animated graphics 194
animated video
creating, Wideo used 189-191
anti-aliasing
vector graphics rendering, improving 237-242
API 252
Application Programming Interface. *See* **API**
area charts
working with 92-96
astroviewer
URL 67

Audacity 140
Audacity software
URL, for downloading 141
audio
recording, from microphone 141-145
recording, permitting to students 158, 159
audiobook
embedding, LibriVox used 154-157

B

bar chart
creating, with hyperlinks 86-90
Bing Maps 3D
stars, watching through 57-60
URL 57
Bing! Maps 3D
URL 62
bitmap graphic 193
bitmap images
vector graphics, converting to 224-227
bitmaps
converting, to vector graphics 227-230
Box.net
about 250
URL 250
working with 254, 256
Box.net API 250
Box.Net Application Programming Interface.
See **Box.Net API**
Box.net repository
enabling 250-253
bridges
on Seine river, URL 53

C

choice activity
used, for graph designing 85, 86
cloze
creating, with pictures 8-12
updating, in Moodle 12, 13
collaborative wiki
designing 125-130
collaborative writing exercises
developing, with Google Docs 110-112
color curves
editing 204-206
column charts
inserting 78-80
constellation maps
working with 66-68

D

digital portfolio. *See* **e-portfolio**
donut interactive chart
drawing 99-101
Dropbox
folder, sharing from 134-136
URL 134

E

effects
adding 206-208
electronic portfolio. *See* **e-portfolio**
e-portfolio 250
European bridges
locating, Google Maps used 53, 54
external image files
linking, from thinglink.com 216-219

F

Fakebook of William Shakespeare
embedding 37-41
File download portfolio
enabling 265-268
files
sharing, with Office 365 Education 130-133
files and folders
uploading 136-138

filters
applying 206-208
Flickr
URL 113, 257
working with 260-263
Flickr images
using, in OpenOffice documents 113-116
Flickr repository
enabling 256-260
folder
sharing, from Dropbox 134-136
free clipart
URL 14

G

gauge chart
creating 104-107
GIMP 2.6.8
URL, for installing 195
Google Docs
about 81
collaborative writing exercises, developing
110-112
URL 110
Google Drive Voice Comments
using, for online assignments 121-125
Google Earth
URL 71
Google Maps
URL 47-50
using, to locate European bridges 53, 54
Google user account
URL 48
Graph designing
choice activity used 85, 86

H

Hot Potatoes
about 8
URL, for downloading 8
hyperlinks
bar chart, creating with 86-90
inserting, into images 90, 91
scalable vector graphics, enhancing with 245-
248

I

images
  embedding, from thinglink.com 220-222
  external image files, linking from thinglink.com 216-220
  hyperlinks, inserting 90, 91
  uploading to, Moodle 211-213
Imagespike
  URL 200
interactive user experiences
  creating 7

J

JClic 8
JClic author
  about 29
  URL, for downloading 24
JClic author 0.2.0.5 24
JCloze 8
JMatch 29

K

kidsastronomy
  URL 68

L

LibriVox
  URL 155
  used, for embedding audiobook 154-157
line chart
  embedding 81-84
lossy
  and lossless compression schemes, selecting between 194-197
Louvre
  URL 212

M

map chart
  designing 102-104
maps
  of Mars, embedding 68-70
  regions, drawing 47, 48

  using, with sceneries 45-47
matching activities
  designing, with pictures 24-28
microphone
  audio, recording from 141-145
Microsoft Excel
  URL 86
Mini-AstroViewer icon
  URL 67
Moodle
  cloze activity, updating 12, 13
  images, uploading to 211-213
  PDF documents, including 117-119
  story, embedding 35-37
  used, for embedding presentation in VoiceThread, 152-154
Moodle course
  3D maps drawing, 3DVIA Shape for Maps used 61-66
  Alfresco repository, enabling 271-273
  Alfresco repository, working with 268-271
  animated 3D graphics, creating 213-216
  animated video creating, Wideo used 189-191
  area charts, working with 92-96
  audiobook embedding, LibriVox used 154-157
  audio, recording from microphone 141-145
  bar charts, creating with hyperlinks 86-90
  bitmaps, converting to vector graphics 227-230
  Box.net repository, enabling 250-253
  Box.net, working with 254-256
  cloze, creating with pictures 8-12
  collaborative wiki, designing 125-130
  collaborative writing exercises, developing with Google Docs 110-112
  color curves, editing 204-206
  column charts, inserting 78-80
  converted vector drawing, parts rendering 230-234
  constellation maps, working with 66, 67
  donut interactive chart, creating 99-101
  effects, adding 206-208
  external image files, linking from thinglink.com 216-222

Fakebook of William Shakespeare, embedding 37-41

File download portfolio, enabling 265-268

files and folders, uploading 136-138

files, sharing with Office 365 Education 130-133

file, uploading 116

filters, applying 206-208

Flickr images, using in OpenOffice documents 113-116

Flickr repository, enabling 256-260

Flickr, working with 260-263

folder, sharing from Dropbox 134-136

gauge chart, creating 104-107

Google Drive Voice Comments, using for online assignments 121-125

Google Maps, using to locate European bridges 53, 54

hotspots, adding to photos 200-204

interactive documents, integrating 109, 110

interactive user experiences, creating 7

line chart, embedding 81-84

lossy and lossless compression schemes, selecting between 194-197

maps, using with sceneries 45-47

map chart, designing 102-104

map of Mars, embedding 68, 70

matching activities, designing with pictures 24-27

moon, labeling 71-73

old photo effect, applying to photo 209

paragraphs, ordering with related scenes 29-31

photos, resizing to appropriate size 197-199

playlist, creating 186-188

podcast creating, SoundCloud used 145-149

podcast embedding, SoundCloud used 145-149

poll, creating 96-99

portfolios, enabling 263, 265

presentation, embedding in VoiceThread 152, 154

Prezi presentation, creating 183-186

quandary maze activity, developing with images 21-23

regions, drawing within map 47-50

scalable vector graphics, embedding 235-237

scalable vector graphics, enhancing with hyperlinks 245-247

stars, watching through Bing Maps 3D 57-60

storyboards, creating 31-35

students, permitting to record audio 158, 159

surface chart, designing 97-99

True/False quiz, designing 13-20

universe, watching 73, 74

vector graphics, converting to bitmap images 224-227

vector graphics, including in Open Office documents 239-242

vector graphics, including in PDF file 244, 245

vector graphics rendering, improving with anti-aliasing 237-239

video editing, YouTube editor used 167-173

video, enhancing with comments 179-182

video, recording 162-164

video, uploading on YouTube 165-167

Vimeo video, embedding 173-178

VoiceThread, using to record presentations 149-151

weather maps, using 50-53

writing activity, creating 28

Yahoo! Maps, working with 55, 57

moon
labeling 71-73

N

Nobel Prize winner
URL 8

O

Office 365 Education
files, sharing with 130-133
URL 131
Office Online Clip Art & Media
URL 9
old photo effect
applying, to photo 209, 210

online assignments
 Google Drive Voice Comments, using 121-125
OpenOffice documents
 Flickr images, using 113-116
 vector graphic, including 239-243
OpenOffice spreadsheet
 URL 86

P

paragraphs
 ordering, with related scenes 29-31
PDF documents
 including, in Moodle 117-119
PDF files
 vector graphics, including 244, 245
photo
 hotspots, adding 200-204
 old photo effect, applying to photo 209, 210
 resizing, to appropriate size 197-199
pictures
 used, for creating cloze 8-12
 used, for designing matching activities 24-28
playlist
 creating 186-188
podcast
 creating, SoundCloud used 145-148
 embedding, SoundCloud used 145-148
poll
 creating 96-99
portfolios
 enabling 263, 265
presentations
 embedding in VoiceThread, Moodle used 152-154
 recording, VoiceThread used 149-152
Prezi
 URL 183
Prezi presentation
 creating 183-186

Q

Quandary 2
 about 8, 21, 22
 URL 21

quandary maze activity
 creating, with images 21-23
 developing, Quandary 2 used 21-23

R

regions
 drawing, within maps 47-50

S

scalable vector graphics
 embedding 235-237
 enhancing, with hyperlinks 245-247
sceneries
 maps, using with 45-47
solar system
 URL 74
SoundCloud
 URL 145
 used, for creating podcast 145-148
 used, for embedding podcast 145-148
stars
 watching, through Bing Maps 3D 57-60
story
 embedding, in Moodle 35-37
storyboards
 creating 31-35
 URL 31
students
 permitting, to record audio 158, 159
surface chart
 designing 97-99
SVG (Scalable Vector Graphics) 223, 224

T

Testmoz
 URL 19
thinglink.com
 external image files, linking from 216-219
 images, embedding from 220, 221
True/False quiz
 designing 13-17
 designing, Hot Potatoes used 18
 designing, Testmoz used 19, 20
 working 17

U

universe
watching 73, 74

V

vector drawing
converted, parts rendering of 230-234
Vector Magic
URL 228
vector graphics
bitmaps, converting to 227-230
converting, to bitmap images 224-227
including, in Open Office documents 239-242
including, in PDF files 244, 245
vector graphics rendering
improving, with anti-aliasing 237-239
video
animated video creating, Wideo used 189-191
editing, YouTube editor used 167-173
enhancing, with comments 179-182
recording 162-164
uploading, on YouTube 165-167
Vimeo
URL 174
Vimeo video
embedding 173-179
VLC media player
URL 162

VoiceThread
presentation embedding, Moodle used 152-154
URL 149
using, to record presentations 149-152

W

weather maps
using 50-53
Wideo
URL 189
used, for creating animated video 189-191
wiki
creating 84
WikiSpaces
URL 125
Wirewax
URL 179
writing activity
creating 28

Y

Yahoo! Maps
URL 55
working with 55
Yeti 111
YouTube
video, uploading on 165-167
YouTube editor
used, for editing video 167-173

Thank you for buying
Moodle 2.5 Multimedia Cookbook
Second Edition

About Packt Publishing

Packt, pronounced 'packed', published its first book "*Mastering phpMyAdmin for Effective MySQL Management*" in April 2004 and subsequently continued to specialize in publishing highly focused books on specific technologies and solutions.

Our books and publications share the experiences of your fellow IT professionals in adapting and customizing today's systems, applications, and frameworks. Our solution based books give you the knowledge and power to customize the software and technologies you're using to get the job done. Packt books are more specific and less general than the IT books you have seen in the past. Our unique business model allows us to bring you more focused information, giving you more of what you need to know, and less of what you don't.

Packt is a modern, yet unique publishing company, which focuses on producing quality, cutting-edge books for communities of developers, administrators, and newbies alike. For more information, please visit our website: www.packtpub.com.

About Packt Open Source

In 2010, Packt launched two new brands, Packt Open Source and Packt Enterprise, in order to continue its focus on specialization. This book is part of the Packt Open Source brand, home to books published on software built around Open Source licenses, and offering information to anybody from advanced developers to budding web designers. The Open Source brand also runs Packt's Open Source Royalty Scheme, by which Packt gives a royalty to each Open Source project about whose software a book is sold.

Writing for Packt

We welcome all inquiries from people who are interested in authoring. Book proposals should be sent to author@packtpub.com. If your book idea is still at an early stage and you would like to discuss it first before writing a formal book proposal, contact us; one of our commissioning editors will get in touch with you.

We're not just looking for published authors; if you have strong technical skills but no writing experience, our experienced editors can help you develop a writing career, or simply get some additional reward for your expertise.

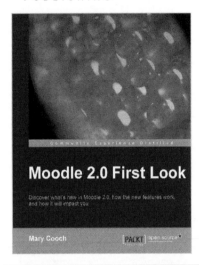

Moodle JavaScript Cookbook

ISBN: 978-1-84951-190-2   Paperback: 180 pages

Over 50 recipes for making your Moodle system more dynamic and responsive with JavaScript

1. Learn why, where, and how to add to add JavaScript to your Moodle site

2. Get the most out of Moodle's built-in extra—the Yahoo! User Interface Library (YUI)

3. Explore a wide range of modern interactive features, from AJAX to Animation

4. Integrate external libraries like jQuery framework with Moodle

History Teaching with Moodle 2

ISBN: 978-1-84951-404-0   Paperback: 280 pages

Create a History course in Moodle packed with lessons and activities to make learning and teaching History interactive and fun

1. Follow the creation of a history course that includes activities for all age groups, with subjects ranging from the medieval times up to the fall of the Third Reich

2. Make your students' homework more exciting by enabling them to watch videos of historical documentaries, participate in group discussions, and complete quizzes from home

3. Save time by transforming your existing lesson plans into interactive courses

Please check **www.PacktPub.com** for information on our titles

Printed in Great Britain
by Amazon.co.uk, Ltd.,
Marston Gate.